ABOUT THE AUTHORS

FRANCIS J. KELLY graduated from Harvard Business School in 1983. A graduate of Amherst College, he spent three years with Young & Rubicam, Inc., before attending Harvard Business School and also worked for Goldman Sachs & Co. on the road to his Harvard MBA. Mr. Kelly is currently an Account Supervisor with the HBM/Creamer Inc advertising agency in Boston.

HEATHER MAYFIELD KELLY, who also graduated from Harvard Business School in 1983, is a manager/teacher in the Loan Officer Development Program at the Bank of Boston. A graduate of Dartmouth College, she spent three years in New York as a middle market commercial lending officer at Chemical Bank before attending Harvard Business School. After graduating HBS, she worked for Temple, Barker, and Sloane Inc. management consulting firm as a specialist in organizational analysis and planning before joining the Bank of Boston.

Francis and Heather were married shortly after their graduation.

WHAT THEY REALLY TEACH YOU AT THE HARVARD BUSINESS SCHOOL

Francis J. Kelly and
Heather Mayfield Kelly

WARNER BOOKS

A Warner Communications Company

A Warner Communications Company

Printed in the United States of America
First Printing: September 1986
10 9 8 7 6 5 4

Library of Congress Cataloging-in-Publication Data

Kelly, Francis.
        What they really teach you at the Harvard Business
School.

        1. Harvard University.   Graduate School of Business
Administration.   I. Kelly, Heather Mayfield.   II. Title.
HF1134.H4K45   1986   650'.07'117444   86-11121

ISBN 0-446-38317-1 (U.S.A.) (pbk.)
        0-446-38318-X (Canada) (pbk.)

To our neighbors, who put up with our insane schedule, our late nights and with our lawn going unmowed for weeks at a time.

To our friends, who stayed friendly despite our long absences from the civilized world.

To our families, who gave us the will and the way to make it to and through Harvard Business School.

And to all of our classmates and HBS alumni who have made HBS the world-renowned institution that it is and who made our experience there so rich.

We gratefully acknowledge the help of Jon Zonderman, an excellent writer and a good listener, without whose help this book would not have been written.

CONTENTS

WHAT THEY REALLY TEACH YOU AT THE HARVARD BUSINESS SCHOOL

ORIENTATION

HARVARD BUSINESS SCHOOL AND ITS FIRST-YEAR CURRICULUM

A gently hissing sound broke the silence outside the window of Morris Hall C–11 at 2:00 a.m. the morning of Wednesday, September 9, 1981. Fran Kelly put down his pencil and clicked off his Hewlett-Packard 38C. Not until another 2:00 a.m., weeks later, would curiosity move Fran to stick his head out the window and find that his bedtime signal was not the voice of some fairy godmother, but the sound of a self-timing lawn sprinkler. Tonight he knew only that it was time to go to bed. In six and one-half hours the first class of his Harvard Business School career would start, and he wanted to start things off right by getting at least five hours' sleep.

Fran had spent his first full day at the school reading more than two hundred pages of case material and writing more than forty pages of analysis in preparation for that first day of classes. He had nearly collapsed of exhaustion and fright the previous afternoon carrying armloads of cases to his dorm room from Baker 20, the infamous room where Harvard Business

School students must go at the end of each day to check for new assignments and cases. The tough old ladies behind the counter had dished the materials out like KPs in a military mess hall, throwing it at the students with no chitchat. A few students had violated the one-way decorum of Baker 20 and had nearly been run over going in the out door or vice versa. Those who knew a little more about the Harvard Business School had come to Baker 20 prepared with shopping carts and dollies at the ready to haul their cases away. But Fran had depended on his own not-so-muscular arms, atrophied by three years in New York City working seventy-hour, six-day weeks as a young account executive with a large advertising agency.

He awoke at seven, took a hot shower, fixed himself a fast cup of coffee and ran off toward Aldrich Hall, where all HBS classes are held. The question that had been the talk of his group of new acquaintances since they arrived on campus two days before still perplexed him: where to sit in the classically designed amphitheater that would be their lecture room.

The eighty-five students who make up each section of HBS's 780-member class have nowhere to hide. Each lecture hall is five rows deep, with about twenty seats to a row, divided into left, right, and center by two aisles. Each section of eighty-five students remains in one classroom for all its classes during the first year. Students usually remain for at least a month in the seat they choose the first day. Since class performance counts for between 25 and 50 percent of each student's course grade, depending on the predilections of the individual professor, securing a choice seat on the first day is a project carried out with the Harvard Business School students' characteristic ferocity.

"Air time," the time to speak and get one's point across, is at a premium in an HBS class, which resembles nothing so much as a commodity pit, with eighty-five future corporate giants clamoring to be heard. In this situation, air time averages less than one minute per student in any class. Taking away the fifteen to twenty minutes that a professor expects from the student who "opens" the discussion, there remains only one hour in which to pick a spot and make an argument. To have spent many hours preparing a case only to get shut out in class can leave one drained, feeling almost abused.

If a student sits high in the amphitheater, he or she may be out of a given professor's line of sight; too low and the student is right in the professor's lap; far to the right or left is outside of a professor's peripheral vision and students there are rarely called on.

Fran was unsure where to sit, but he was damned sure he was going to get to his classroom early enough to give himself options. He felt a little like a jerk as he walked across the business school campus at 7:30 on a bright, fall morning, heading for a class that was an hour away from beginning. The Charles River shone blue, reflecting the sky; the air was crisp and clean. But all Fran could think about was maximizing HBS air time. As he made his way across the stately campus he made his fateful decision: He would go to the middle of the front row and challenge those professors on their own ground.

Fran was mildly surprised to notice a few others walking toward Aldrich; nearing the door to his section's room, he was even surprised to hear a buzz of voices coming from inside the amphitheater. As he opened the door, he realized that although he was forty-five minutes early, he was also too late! This was The Harvard Business School. The room was already two-thirds full, and the choice seats were taken. Only a James Worthy-style drive across the room secured Fran the last available seat in the center section.

One woman had set up shop the night before. She had left her name card and notebook on her seat, and had then gone home for a night's sleep. An entire study group, formed during the introductory cook-out the night before, had arrived before 7:30 to take up a strategic row. Several number-cruncher types were huddled around a large electric outlet multi-plug in the back of the room, their calculators plugged in and humming. One guy in the last row was even setting up a personal computer—which he was later forced to remove.

Fran dropped his case materials in amazement and headed

to The Pub for another cup of coffee. In line, he noticed a short, thick-lensed student reading and underlining a case Fran had apparently overlooked the night before. Panic struck. After all that work, a day of reading, analyzing and note-taking, had he read the wrong cases? Wide-eyed, he shook the young man from behind and croaked, "What case is that?" Straightening his LaCoste shirt, the young man calmly explained that, given his possession of a 150 IQ, a personal computer prestocked with a data base of the cases from the previous year, and his professional experience as a consultant, he was already reading *next week's* cases. Fran experienced his first case of HBS morning sickness.

Francis J. Kelly III knew he was at The Harvard University Graduate School of Business Administration, the infamous *B* school. And he knew it was going to be a long two years. One small coffee and one shaken ego in hand, he headed back toward Aldrich Hall.

The Harvard University Graduate School of Business Administration has been called many things, but in polite society it is called Harvard Business School. Many consider it the premier American school for graduate-level business education. Whether or not HBS offers the best graduate business education is not as important, so argues the school itself, as the fact that it is a unique experience that produces fabulously successful graduates. By others, the school is also considered to be a haven for The Establishment and a proven way to beat into its sons and daughters the skills and values they will need to stay on top and maintain their privileged status in society.

We—Fran and Heather Kelly—weren't happy all the time in our two years at HBS. In fact, we were completely miserable much of the time, during the 1981–83 school years, when we both attended the school. We didn't love being tired and irritable, constantly under extreme stress, and pressured to be overcompetitive for much of two full years. We especially didn't love being automatically stamped "HBS assholes" by many people upon our graduation. However, we do strongly believe that the HBS experience is unique, worthwhile, and highly rewarding for the right people. Most important, we think not enough is said of the Harvard Business School curriculum itself.

In the pages that follow, we will try to give readers a feel for what they really do teach at the Harvard Business School, at least in the first year, when all students take Harvard's prescribed ten-course curriculum. We will focus only on the first year, because in the second year students have a choice of dozens of courses that help them specialize in different areas of business and management. In the first year, however, the courses are uniform to ensure that each HBS student has gained a common body of knowledge.

But in order to explain what the courses are about in more than a dry, academic sense, we need first to impart something of the flavor of the Harvard Business School environment—the constant pressure from September to June, the brilliant classmates, the tough, demanding teachers; the making and defending of countless decisions day after day; and the driving effort to master a process of analysis that can be applied successfully to virtually any business situation.

Many readers will, with some justification, accuse us of cutting the heart out of the painstakingly developed HBS courses, but in these ten relatively brief chapters we believe we are able to give an accurate overview of what is taught in each course.

This book is a curricular summary and experiential overview written by two recent grads, before the pain of it has worn off and the nostalgic feeling has settled in. For those who have not been to HBS and are excited by this book, apply. For those who have attended HBS and who think we didn't write the book we should have, please don't contact us. Just go ahead and write it. The HBS story is an incredibly rich one that merits reflecting upon, discussing, and retelling.

It costs a lot to go to Harvard or any other good graduate school these days. Potential students should have a pretty good idea of what to expect before they spend all that dough. This is a what-it's-like-to-be-there book—the kind of book we wish had been available to us when we were thinking about applying to Harvard, Stanford, Tuck, and other business schools back in 1980.

Not that one must be thinking of attending HBS to be able to get something out of understanding the school's program and its analytical methodology.

Wherever we go, people ask what it was like to go to HBS. Yet many misconceptions about the school are abroad, both about the program and about the people who go there. We would like to dispel some of those myths through an honest discussion of what gets taught at HBS and what the environment is really like.

The environment means, above all, the people, and there are many stereotypes about HBS graduates. We often wonder: How did we go in just two short years from being nice, "average Joe" college graduates starting careers in New York City to arrogant, elitist number crunchers on the banks of the Charles River? We don't think we did, but as two hardworking, middle-class folks have recently found out firsthand, it's hard to overcome a strongly entrenched stereotype.

For example, with a degree from Amherst College and two years of excellent advertising agency experience under his belt, Fran decided to test the waters in 1980 by interviewing for a job with another major New York ad agency. He got very positive vibes during the interview and, soon afterward, his first offer from the agency; and even though he kept saying no, the suitor agency called offering him terrific jobs every three months. In 1983, with his new degree from HBS, he reapplied to that firm. When he went in for an interview, he noticed scribbled on his resume a note from the new personnel director to those interviewing Fran: "Looks like another Harvard Business School Asshole." Same applicant. Same love for the advertising business. But now he was an HBS asshole.

Of course, there were consulting firms that would have laughed Fran out the door before HBS but were now offering him $60,000 a year to start, with low-interest loans, exploding bonuses, a personal computer, and the rest. For that kind of money, a lot of people don't mind being stereotyped. But, in a way, those outrageous offers only serve to perpetuate the stereotype.

This stereotype of HBS graduates is also perpetuated by the recent spate of books that, with or without the use of humor, purport to teach people all they need to know about management. Business-school-bashing, and especially HBS-bashing, has become a big-time sport in recent times. Nobody needs to worry whether Harvard Business School will survive the onslaught, but the idea that people attend HBS solely to build and maintain the supposed HBS character type is incorrect and does a disservice to the school and to its highly diverse pool of graduates.

As to the Harvard Business School curriculum, very few people have a clear idea what gets taught at HBS. We strongly believe that a review of the HBS curriculum, even in abbreviated form and without benefit of on-campus experience, can be very valuable to anyone interested in becoming a better business manager.

Americans in general are showing a newfound interest in the American economic and business climate, and indeed in the economic and business climate throughout the world. People are increasingly aware that the health of American business is of great importance to the health and status of the nation as a whole. Because it plays an important role in training this country's business leaders, the Harvard Business School has an important obligation to evaluate continually its offerings, in terms of both style and substance, in order to keep up with the changing needs of the national and international business world.

This book offers a brief look at that program, which often seems shrouded in mystery and secrecy, and opens it up to new analysis and debate. In this way we hope people will come to recognize HBS more for what it is, and will also better understand what it isn't.

Business people who do not have graduate business training

will find enough information on the type of material and the analytic approach taught at HBS so as to be able to apply it in analyzing everyday business situations. An HBS education can't hope to supplant experience, but we hope it can supplement that experience. People considering going to HBS should carefully consider the curriculum before making that jump. Is now the right time in a person's career-development process to tackle an MBA program?

Those who deal with HBS graduates, as colleagues or as competitors, and especially those who hire them can get a better idea of what HBSers probably know or don't know, what they can and can't do when they get out of school. The better one understands both the substance of the HBS curriculum and the thought processes of an HBS graduate, the more effective that person can be at hiring the right Harvard MBAs and integrating them effectively into the organization.

Finally, HBS grads will want to know how the school is changing and what the current first-year course structure looks like. They may also be interested to find out what the HBS environment is like today. In many ways, the environment is much less changed than the curriculum; a terrible thought to some, and one that will bring a knowing smile to many others.

THE HBS PROOF: STUDENTS AND ALUMNI

The individuals who make it through the two years of HBS have proven by the end of the program their desire, potential, intellect, personality, integrity, and achievement.

When the students enroll, the school's environment and curriculum begin to cut away many of the rough edges and greatly accelerate their development as managers and future business leaders. They are exposed to over 700 business cases. They work with dozens of faculty members and are introduced to many prominent business leaders who come to the school each year. The program provides students with the ability to analyze any business situation and develop recommendations using specific analytic tools. In addition, students interact continually with a diverse, highly intelligent and intensely competitive student body. Through immersion in an enormously demanding environment, most students find their motivation galvanized and their self-confidence increased immensely.

Are these claims a little strong? Sure. But the school's track record speaks for itself. A recent survey showed that about 20 percent of the top officers of Fortune 500 companies have degrees from HBS. In addition, about one-third of HBS graduates of twenty-five years ago now hold positions equal to chief executive officer, managing director, partner or owner. Harvard Business School graduates form the backbone of the leading-edge fields of investment banking, venture capital and management consulting. Many current graduates receive starting salaries of more than $60,000. An HBS degree can't turn a turkey into a CEO, but few turkeys finish the program, and the accomplishments of Harvard's alumni are manifest.

OUR METHODOLOGY

There are ten required first-year courses at Harvard Business School. Each is covered in one chapter in this book. Figure 0–1 is an outline of the 1985–86 MBA first-year schedule.

We summarize the courses in an order different from the one in which they are taught at HBS.

We have put the Business Policy course first, although HBS doesn't teach the course until the end of the year, because it is the overview course that gives to students the full scope of a general manager's job. Harvard's reasoning for closing with it is that its first-year students must be firmly grounded in the specific business disciplines before they can hope to command the overview.

After Business Policy comes our chapter on Organizational Behavior. Harvard breaks up the Organizational Behavior class and runs it on both sides of Human Resource Management—a theory, practice, theory series. We feel it is important to get the theoretical framework of Organizational Behavior—which in some ways is all encompassing, as is Business Policy—into

Figure 0–1. First-Year Curriculum and Schedule for Harvard Business School's MBA Program

Course	September	October	November	December	January	February	March	April	May
Control	■	■	■	░	■				
Managerial Economics	■	■	■	░	■				
Marketing			■	░	■	■	■		
Organizational Behavior	■	■	■	░	■				
Management Communication		■	■	░	■				
Human Resource Management						■	■		
Production and Operations Management					■	■	■	■	■
Finance					■	■	■	■	■
Business, Government, and the International Economy							░	■	■
Business Policy							░	■	■
Management Simulation Exercise							░	■	■

the dialogue up front. It shows how "the game" of business—corporate culture, office politics, and the like—gets portrayed at HBS.

Our following two chapters, on Marketing and Finance courses, go together as something of a team. If one thinks of marketing as the engine of a company, then finance is the fuel. Without cash the engine can't run; but an ill-conceived, old-fashioned, or poorly designed marketing engine can't be made efficient by pouring into it all the fuel in the world. In the marketing class, students learn how to develop a product that meets a real need, how to educate the public about the product, and how to get it to those who need it and can afford to purchase it. In Finance, students learn how to maximize a firm's financial strength by building the best possible capital structure, and by making sound investment and finance decisions. The course teaches the analysis of flexibility, income, control, and timing (FRICT analysis).

Cash is one of a company's three major resources. Human and capital resources, the other two, must be managed with as much acumen and sophistication, if not more. These points are demonstrated in the next two chapters, Production and Operations Management, and Human Resource Management. Ninety-five percent of HBS students *do not* go into production. However, contrary to popular opinion, all HBS students learn about that critical part of business. True to the HBS idea of general management, the first of these two courses stresses how and why production and operations decisions must correctly tie in with overall corporate strategy. After all, if you don't produce a good product at the right time in the right quantities for the right price, you usually don't have a viable company. Human Resource Management (HRM) is another area few HBS grads make a career in. Considered a "soft" course, as is Organizational Behavior, HRM is taken somewhat lightly by some. Although these two areas may be orphaned by the hard-core HBS student body, Harvard considers knowledge and skill in these areas integral to the performance of a good general manager.

Learning how to manage a company is only half the battle. The other half is learning how to evaluate the success of that management activity and how to communicate its performance to others both inside and outside the organization. Control, the next course covered, looks at the evaluation, or score-keeping, aspects of management. "Control" of a company lies in the systems, techniques, and procedures for planning, predicting, measuring, and assessing the performance of the whole company or any unit within the company on an ongoing basis.

Managerial Economics is a course that helps students analyze the decision-making process and keep score of individual decisions using various quantification methods. The language of managerial economics allows decision-makers to break down complex decisions into their component parts; to focus on independent elements one at a time; and to develop a logical sequential chain of decisions. It allows managers to predict uncertain events with greater accuracy.

Management Communication is the course in which the HBS student struggles to learn how to take all the analysis, recommendations, and decisions made about a company and communicate them to others, both inside and outside the company. Clear and concise written and oral communication is necessary to make a decision and policies have real impact.

Our final chapter on the HBS curriculum—Business, Government, and the International Economy (BGIE)—examines the corporation as a small component of a vast national and international economic structure. National and world events always both limit and create opportunities for a company, and management must carefully analyze those factors.

Each of these ten chapters is framed around a four-part model. The chapters will not look exactly alike, but these four major questions will be answered in each:

- Who is the decision-maker?
- What types of decisions must be made in each area and what impact do decisions have on the corporation as a whole?

- What types of analytic techniques are taught at HBS for making decisions, and what form should recommendations take to solve specific business problems?
- Finally, how does one do a quick check on a decision before it is implemented to make sure it is the best possible? And how does one conduct a post-decision audit to assess decision-making processes?

We hope that by following this analytic outline for each chapter, readers can take any business situation they face and use the relevant HBS analytical tools as aids to work through the situation and come to well-reasoned recommendations and implementation strategies.

Before moving into our ten chapters, which outline the identically titled HBS course material, we think it is important to give readers a more complete sense of the process by which the material is taught and the environment in which the learning takes place.

A LITTLE HISTORY OF HBS

Founded in 1908, the Harvard Business School was the first graduate school of business that required its students to have a bachelor's degree. The school specifically sought students who did not have technical training or prior training in business subjects, but broad education in the arts and sciences. Indeed, the school was actually founded as a graduate department of the school of arts and sciences.

Over the years the philosophy has modified but not changed radically. Harvard was the first business school to teach business as a profession, like law or medicine. Over three-quarters of a century, the idea of a unified first-year curriculum with specialized courses in the second year has evolved, and is now the model for most graduate business schools.

Originally housed in buildings in Harvard Yard, the Business School currently has its own campus just across the Charles River from Cambridge in the Allston section of Boston.

THE HBS CASE-STUDY METHOD

The curriculum, as we have mentioned before, is structured around the case study. These actual business cases are researched by a team of Harvard faculty, former students and outside researchers. Each case is designed and used to make a specific business point. Usually, one case is read for each of the two or three classes that meet each day. HBS students attend classes five days a week.

In an eighty-minute class, one student is asked to "open" the discussion by presenting the case, analyzing the situation, and recommending an approach to solving the business problem or carrying the company forward toward its stated goals. These openings generally take between ten and twenty minutes.

Then, all hell breaks loose, with eighty-four other students scrambling to argue how they would deal with the situation differently and why their approach would be better. Some teachers gently guide the discussion, others prod, while still others are highly aggressive and intimidating in their questioning.

Harvard Business School cases are different from the cases used elsewhere. In many case-study programs, the cases read include a statement of outcome as part of the case material. The HBS cases are always "incomplete" cases: The outcome is unknown, and important information is often missing. The point of HBS cases is not to read how others solved management problems, but to take a complicated and unresolved situation and determine how it could best be managed. In this way, there is no real "right answer" to a case study, but myriad ways in which one might persuasively argue a situation could be handled. So many variables go into dealing with a business situation that one person's solution may appear to be "wrong" or another person's "right" only because of the subtle difference in the way each handles one aspect. In some ways, solving an HBS case, and getting through Harvard Business School, is like putting together a constantly growing jigsaw puzzle.

The Harvard case method asks that students learn by doing, by putting themselves in the position of managers. In each chapter, that is to say in each of the ten business areas, we briefly introduce you to some of the situations HBS students face in their case studies. One cannot get through a course at HBS by memorizing, only by reading and rigorously analyzing two or three cases each night—each of which usually takes two to four hours to do justice to.

THE SECTION CONCEPT

Another Harvard concept is the first-year section, the group of eighty-five people with whom a student will spend the entire first year. The section is large enough to represent the HBS student body as a whole in its gender and ethnic makeup. A mini-society on the one hand and a large corporate board on the other, the eighty-five students in a section spend the year taking all their classes together, arguing with each other, working in small study groups, socializing, and participating in extracurricular activities with each other. Over the course of a year, eighty-five strangers get to know one another very well.

While similar in many ways, each section takes on a personality of its own. Some sections are intensely competitive, others are supportive. Students in one section with specialized knowledge in accounting may spend their own time preparing a tutorial in organizational control for their classmates. In some sections, students have been known to gang up on less-qualified students, forcing them out of school early—usually between 5 and 10 percent of each section drops out or is forced out in the first year. In other sections, people have worked hard to make sure everyone stays in by making sure that no one student performs badly in more than one or two courses. As in any business or other dynamic organization, leaders gradually emerge in each section and each student seems to find a niche.

THE HBS STUDENT

There are several ways to look at the student body at HBS. One is the statistical breakdown that Harvard compiles, which indicates that the class of 1985 had 785 students, only 23 of whom entered directly from college, 133 of whom were married, 73 of whom were minorities and 196 of whom were women. The vast majority, 76 percent, were between 23 and 26 years of age. Twenty-four percent had been economics majors, and another 24 percent had been engineering majors in undergraduate school. Another 17 percent had been business administration majors. Totaled, 66 percent had been trained in what Harvard originally would have considered a "technical" or "business" discipline. However, others were the products of liberal arts educations—11 percent had backgrounds in the humanities, and 9 percent in the social sciences. Another 10 percent had studied the pure sciences. And the students in the class of 1985 came from more than forty states and more than forty foreign countries.

But there are other, more insightful, ways to profile the HBS student body.

First, they all have been very successful *before* they arrive at HBS. Most graduated at the very top of their undergraduate classes. Before entering HBS, most have had between one and three years of highly successful full-time work experience and have demonstrated basic business acumen as well as academic strength.

Second, the HBS students are almost all extremely competitive, ambitious, and highly motivated individuals. Heated discussion, if not outright argument, comes as second nature to many.

And third, HBS students almost all have good-sized, if not oversized, egos. Having been big fish in undergraduate life, and having been considered great prospects in their jobs after college, they often need to have others recognize just what kind of superstar they really are in order to stay motivated. Students at HBS attain a high degree of self-confidence,

FIGURE 0–2. MBA Class Profiles—Classes of 1985, 1986

	1985	1986
Class Size:	785	780
Students entering directly from college	3.0%	3.0%
Women	25.0	24.0
Minority	9.3	9.0
International	12.7	14.0
Married	16.9	20.0
One or more children	3.3	3.0
Age at Admission:		
Under 23	1.9	3.0
23–24	43.7	41.0
25–26	33.0	34.0
27–28	12.6	14.0
29 and over	8.8	8.0
	100	100
College Majors:		
Business Administration	17.2	18.0
Economics	23.8	24.0
Engineering	24.1	23.0
Government	4.4	5.0
Humanities	11.1	12.0
Pure Science	10.7	9.0
Social Science	8.7	9.0
	100	100

sometimes more than bordering on hubris. But in some ways that's understandable: For two years they have been beaten down, then puffed up, told that after they have survived Harvard they can afford to consider themselves the best young management talent the country has to offer.

During their second year, many HBS students have their egos massaged by investment banks and consulting firms who make offers of $50,000 or $60,000 in starting salary, plus bonuses, for these newly minted whiz kids to join their firms.

But the pressure is intense, and the drive to succeed often so strong that people lose sight of their goal—if indeed they have one—and concentrate on competing with other students to see who can get the most lucrative offers from the companies with the biggest names.

We had to endure the guy with the thick glasses from the first day's coffee line; he who was a week ahead, then two weeks ahead, then three weeks ahead, and he always vaguely remembered the case we mortals were working on when we ran into him. It was always an easy problem.

We had to live with the insensitive character who would offer up at least one quantitative analysis each week that only he and the professor understood even remotely. Eighty-four others listened with quizzical expressions on their faces while he rattled off equations and numbers and the professor scribbled it all down. There was, of course, no explanation given to the rest of us. Of course, we did nod knowingly despite our confusion.

We had to listen at least once a day as the star performers who came to HBS from the world's most prestigious investment banks reminded us, from behind locked jaws, of their previous employer's name.

We had to watch mediocre tennis players—mostly second-year students—troop off to the courts in their very-white whites, hauling an average of 2.6 tennis racquets per person.

But for each of these types, we met two others who spoke quietly, kept their egos mostly in check and went calmly about the business of grinding through the learning opportunity that HBS offered—people who could make you laugh in the most tense situations, who could make some sense out of the most confusing business problems, who offered up their refreshing perspectives in straightforward discussion. Such people predominated in the amphitheaters at HBS and often relegated the unsavories to a backseat.

Whatever their airs and idiosyncrasies, most HBS students are bright, motivated, successful, and competitive *before* making it to HBS. And it is in the day-in and day-out interaction with this high-caliber student body that one of the greatest learning and growing experiences of the HBS years takes place.

Two years of facing nothing but the most challenging competition has to raise one's confidence level when the time comes to go out and meet the challenges found in the real business world.

UNIVERSAL CHARACTER TYPES

It's a feature of corporate life—and the HBS classroom—that different people attack problems in consistently different ways. By February or March of the first year, one can almost guess what is going to come out of Debbie or Ted or Ray each time he or she speaks, because one has come to know how each one thinks, talks, and fits into the group.

As in most real-world business environments, certain people think in certain ways. Consider what happens in any company. The right way to convince Horace that one deserves a new window office may be altogether the wrong story to use if one wants to impress Dexter, and may in fact result in a lightless cubicle if Fred hears it. Over the course of a year spent battling to communicate and persuade in an HBS section, students learn an awful lot about the importance of knowing an audience and recognizing the different character types that make it up.

At least six character types contributed to every case discussion in our HBS '83 sections. From talking to many alumni from previous years it seems clear those types have been well represented in every HBS debate.

1. *The Quantitative Analysis Jock:* This character helps give HBS its bad name. Although worth his or her weight in gold on Wall Street, in a classroom the QA Jock can bore everyone to tears—and in the real world, can easily irritate and intimidate associates. This character thrives on numbers and equations. All data, including numerous irrelevancies, must be gathered and incorporated into an analysis before any decision can be made. The QA Jock has a personal computer before

setting foot on campus at HBS (all students currently must buy one when they arrive) and has created a data base of cases over the summer before entering the classroom for the first time. Finance and control are this person's strong suits.

2. *The Humanist:* The opposite of the Quantitative Analysis Jock, the Humanist is more concerned with human feelings than with quantitative data, and will avoid quantitative analysis at all costs. This person thrives on the "soft" courses—Organizational Behavior and Human Resource Management.

3. *The Synthesizer:* Aware of both numbers and feelings, and their political implications, this person specializes in building consensus, mediating, and telling people they are "saying the same thing in two different ways." The Synthesizer often forms an opinion after all others have had a crack at it, and "sums up." Favorite courses are "big picture" studies like BGIE and Business Policy.

4. *The Political Animal:* There is not much original thinking here but great sensitivity to the politics of every situation is evident. This person is aggressive and confident, and often brilliantly restates others' ideas. The Political Animal is good at saying what the boss (or professor) wants to hear and what the boss often wishes he himself had said. The Political Animal, as we know too well from our real world experience, can survive and thrive almost anywhere, but tends to shy away from courses requiring heavy number crunching.

5. *The Skydecker:* Sitting along the upper tier of the HBS amphitheater, relaxed and above the political fray in the pit, this character tends to be relaxed, but can play an active role in prodding the class when necessary. Like a backbencher in a parliamentary government, the Skydecker carefully picks spots to swoop down on out of the heavens to make a broad but often original point.

6. *The Eccentric:* At first, it seems a pure mistake of nature that this person is at Harvard, or in business at all. But

the Eccentric adds yet another perspective, a grittiness and savvy that a lot of others in the class lack. On looking back, many others will say the eccentric enriched everyone's experience at HBS.

To be effective, HBS students are forced to study how all character types react to any given situation or case. Watching how people interact is important. From dealing with all of the various character types, one begins to learn the art of communicating appropriately to persuade people with very different viewpoints of the validity of yours. That's a vital lesson to take into the business world from the HBS section arrangement and case-study method.

LIKE A BLAST FURNACE

The Harvard case system makes for a continuous pressure-cooker environment. Since classroom participation counts for between 25 and 50 percent of each class grade, there is intense pressure to prepare for every class.

A palpable fear reigns over the room as the professor scans the class at the beginning of a session to "cold call" on a student to open the discussion. To be cold-called and to have to "pass" because one has not done the analysis is one of the great Harvard faux pas. To "pass" means that a grade will automatically be lowered, and passing once too often could mean flunking a class, no matter how well one does on the two exams for that class. Failing three or more classes is enough to force one, in the HBS vernacular, to "hit the screen" and risk flunking out. A three-tier system is used to grade each class—the top 15 percent get E (excellent), the middle 70 to 75 percent get SAT (satisfactory), and the bottom 10 to 15 percent get LP, or low pass (pronounced loop).

It is black comedy at its best to see eighty-five hard-driving, egomaniacal mega-top-notchers coughing, dropping pens, running hands through their hair and generally trying to duck out of sight as a professor scans the class while deciding whom to nominate that particular day for the Spanish Inquisition. It's equally amusing to see how once someone has begun a presentation, the same eighty-five—minus one—now instantly know exactly what the student who opened is doing wrong, how it should be done right, and why the presenter is in general a turkey.

The moment the poor schlepp who opens finishes, pale and sweating, hands shoot up and the fight for air time begins.

Many HBS students have little contact with the faculty and administration outside class, and if one gets sick during the semester—that's tough. It's the student's job to keep up, period.

HBS is a pressure-cooker environment that teaches not only a lot about business analysis, but also about working hard, working fast, working independently, making decisions, defending decisions, and otherwise looking out for one's self. Even though students spend a lot of time interacting with others—in class, or outside in study groups, on group projects, and in the dorms comparing notes—students are taught to be self-reliant.

The HBS message is clear: The HBS student has the capability to get the job done; to see the big picture; to do the analysis; to decide what is important and what isn't in a complex situation; to make the decisions and make the recommendations that need to be made even though one never has all the information one would like. Finally, there is never just one right answer, and everyone will make a share of mistakes along the way. And whenever, somehow, one emerges covered in glory, there is little time for basking in it. Get ready for tomorrow, when the process starts all over again.

ANOTHER WELCOME TO HARVARD BUSINESS SCHOOL

How tough is the environment at HBS? The perspective provided by the following story may seem skewed, but the story is true. It happened one afternoon in the fall of 1981 in a Section D versus Section H intramural soccer match.

Fran Kelly, a very unheralded soccer forward, knew he was hurt the second he kicked wildly for the soccer ball and collided with the man from Section D who had arrived on the loose ball at the same moment.

It was an unusually competitive game between two sections. With midterms only a few days away, the students were taking out some of their frustrations on the soccer ball.

Fran's team was behind three to nothing with only a few minutes left in the game when the collision and the sickening thud occurred. It was an unmistakable sound, audible to the goalie at the far end of the field and the small group of fans on the sidelines. Fran cartwheeled through the air and landed on his back, with his right leg bent underneath him, both bones above the right ankle broken clean through.

The pain was intense as Fran waited for the ambulance a teammate had called. Any movement hurt badly so it didn't take much analysis to conclude that he shouldn't be moved. Darkness was rapidly approaching, the blue November sky turning a deep purple and the air quickly cooling. A friend laid a jacket over Fran's shoulders; the somber group continued to wait for the ambulance to make its way across the river from Cambridge.

Suddenly, one of the players from Section D broke through the huddle of HBSers around Fran and muttered, "We'd better get him off the field, it's getting dark." A couple of sets of hands quickly led the man away.

A few minutes later the guy was back. "I mean it, we gotta move this guy. It's practically dark and I don't have time to replay this game another day," he screamed. Fran tried to roll over, but his right ankle didn't roll with him. His roommate, Scott, shook his head in disbelief and physically removed the other player from the area.

Three minutes later, the man charged through the crowd again, now visibly upset and determined to be heard. He looked down at Fran, shook his finger at the wounded man and delivered his ultimatum: "Okay, fella, if you're not going to move, your team is going to have to forfeit the game and I want you to know it." It looked like a rugby scrum as the astonished group pulled the man away for the final time.

HBS is not known for its warmth.

Harvard's reaction to Fran's broken leg, which put him in the hospital and out of class for eight days, was simple: tough. The school's biggest concern was that the ambulance had taken him to a private hospital and not to the Harvard infirmary.

Well, they say nothing good ever comes easy in life. Reading through the academic course material summarized in the next ten chapters, keep in mind the method by which it is delivered and the environment in which it gets taught to appreciate fully *What They Really Teach You at the Harvard Business School*.

1

BUSINESS POLICY

Business Policy, known to the Harvard Business School student simply as BP, could be called the cornerstone of the HBS curriculum. It is the only two-year course that has a Part I, taken in the first year; and a Part II, which is mandatory in the second year. In Business Policy I, HBS students look at the functions and responsibilities of general managers in formulating corporate strategies and policies. In Business Policy II, students concentrate on learning how to implement corporate strategy once it has been developed.

It is logical that we start with Business Policy in looking at the HBS curriculum. HBS prides itself on the development of this course, which many other business schools now copy to some extent. The course puts students in management roles, often president or CEO, and asks them to determine the overall direction a business will take.

Business Policy deals with the "big, big picture," the construction of an all-encompassing corporate strategy, and the subsequent development of specific policies to help the company reach its strategic goals. These policies must take into account all areas of the business, including corporate structure, manufacturing, marketing, finance, accounting, human resources, risk management, internal and external communications, and government relations. In short, Business Policy provides a model of business management thinking that will be covered in depth in the other nine first-year HBS courses.

Business Policy is a Synthesizer's dream course. It entails piecing together a course of action based on analysis of an enormous amount of information drawn from many business disciplines. Quantitative Analysis Jocks do well in some aspects of Business Policy, using their skills to determine how a company is currently performing and which options it has open to it in the future. Students with other types of personalities also find they are comfortable with aspects of the Business Policy curriculum.

In this chapter, as in all the following chapters, we will go through the four-stage process outlined in chapter 1.

For Business Policy, the four steps of the analysis are—

- To understand the role of the general manager
- To understand the idea of corporate strategy and why it is so important, as well as the difference between corporate strategy and business policy
- To outline various methods of analyzing corporate strategy and business policy issues—including industry analysis, competitor analysis, and analysis of one's own firm—as a means of developing sound business policy recommendations
- Finally, to develop a quick checklist for evaluating the effectiveness of a corporate strategy.

At the end of each chapter, we will provide a group of five or six key questions to ask about any organization so that readers will be able to do a simple, fast HBS-style analysis of their own business or of any business situation.

What HBS students do in BP, in effect, is to develop a corporate strategy selection process that includes determining what strategy options exist and which of those are realistic; what limitations are placed on the corporation by personal and societal expectations; and what is required to balance short-term and long-term objectives when setting up a strategy and policies. Using a number of different analytical tools HBS students learn to develop a coherent business analysis that enables them to understand better a company's current competitive position, as well as how that position may be enhanced, and what policies must be introduced throughout the company to attain desired results.

To a great extent, this ability to boil down any business situation to a set of key questions that lead to sensible recommendations is the essence of what HBS seeks to give its students. The questions asked vary depending upon the area of business being studied, but the overall analytic process is the same.

Looking at the big picture in an organization is something everyone can do to some degree, but seeing that picture quickly and plucking the *important* elements out of it to incorporate into analysis is something that comes from training, practice, and practical experience. The HBS experience gives students the first two elements of this triumvirate—training and practice. Though almost all HBS students have two to six years of work experience before entering Harvard, they only gain real practical experience once they leave HBS and begin applying what they have learned.

The HBS experience is no substitute for on-the-job experience, but it provides a foundation that gives a hardworking, levelheaded person with sensitivity, self-confidence, and a desire to achieve the capability to become a fine manager.

THE BUSINESS POLICY DECISION-MAKER

In the Business Policy course, students learn by reading thirty to thirty-five cases, as they do in each of their HBS classes.

In BP, they are asked to put themselves in the position of various corporate leaders, as in the following examples:

- The head of a major U.S. auto manufacturer facing the onslaught of the Japanese auto companies in the early 1980s
- The head of a small regional brewery fighting for survival in the late 1970s against major national breweries, such as Miller Brewing Company and Anheuser-Busch
- The head of an international pharmaceutical manufacturer confronting increasingly varied forms of government regulation in the various countries around the globe in which it markets and produces its products
- The head of a U.S. tobacco firm earning record profits but facing mounting government and consumer concerns over the health risks of its major product.

These four situations provide wildly different issues that the student must confront. Acting out the role of a senior general manager in these situations illustrates in a real way the best and the worst of the HBS education.

After thinking about these management issues for two years and reading cases that each pose a similar, yet somewhat different major issue, the HBS graduate has a broad foundation of knowledge and theory from which to work. But classroom generals do not have to make split-second decisions that involve large sums of real money and affect real people's lives. HBS graduates must guard against a false sense of business reality. In addition, there is a tendency on the part of some graduates to get frustrated easily when hired by large companies and put into an entry-level position. Once one has tasted the executive suite, even if it's only in the classroom, it is naturally a bit frustrating to take a cubicle in the back room.

THE ROLE OF THE GENERAL MANAGER

Harvard Business School prides itself on training general managers. The school's goal is to be the premier source of men and women with the talent and the training to become excellent general managers in any and all fields of business. An important part of the Business Policy course is to explain the full role of the general manager to these students.

Unfortunately, the concept of general management as it is taught at Harvard is often misunderstood. While Harvard sees general management as an important and rewarding career, many in the business world think of general managers as inefficient, jack-of-all-trades-but-master-of-none types. We strongly believe the Harvard concept is sound. As with so many things, bad general managers have created a negative stereotype of general management and many of the misconceptions have never been cleared up—a case where maybe even HBS has failed with its corporate communication.

Many Harvard-trained MBAs develop into ideal candidates for chief executive officer of a company because they have been trained to see things from the perspective of the CEO, to see the running of any operating area within a company in terms of that area's impact on the company as a whole.

But an HBS-trained individual need not head a company to be a valuable part of it. General management skills are needed to direct a 2-person department or a 5,000-employee division. It is a matter of keeping the goals and strategies of the company clearly in view, then setting policies at the level on which one operates to ensure that those strategies get put into action every day.

Business Policy cases illustrate that good general managers know that no account, product group, office, or division of a company is a personal fiefdom, but a subunit of an enterprise that must present a consistent, coherent policy to employees and customers. In many companies goals are not well communicated to those below the ranks of senior management. Although this cuts down on the effectiveness of any manager, a good general manager will be able to extrapolate from what is known about the corporate strategy in order to communicate that strategy to staff members, suppliers, customers, and to the public at large.

Decisions made by the president of a company affect all managers, from the manager of production facilities to the manager of the mail room. Although not many HBS graduates start in the mail room, their HBS training would not be lost if they did. Decisions are made every day in the mail room, and the better the mail-room head understands where the company is trying to go, the more likely it will be that the department will be able to assist the company in reaching those goals.

One begins to see in Business Policy analysis why even many nonmanagers can benefit from a broad business perspective. Specialists educated as general managers are often more aware of how their area of interest affects and is affected by other areas of the company. Consultants, either appointed from in-house or hired from outside management-consulting firms, should have the broadest possible education and experience in order to advise their clients effectively. This is also true of outside board members. General managers who sit on the board, who have faced a number of situations in their business careers and who have read about them in the course of their business education, often possess a valuable perspective on the formulation and implementation of corporate strategy—a perspective that is not present when managers are involved on a minute-by-minute basis with nitty-gritty issues in their own special areas of concern.

In addition, the skills and perspective gained at HBS can also be transferred from the business world to the management of government, quasi-governmental and nonprofit organizations. While only a decade ago business, government, and the not-for-profit sectors were considered to be three truly different entities with fundamentally different modes of operation, each sector is now seen by most as an integral and closely interrelated component of our culture and economy—each requiring the same managerial skills and knowledge in order to function successfully.

SAILING THE CORPORATE SHIP

The analogy of a general manager being like the skipper of a sailing ship is an apt one. In order to win a sailing race, everything has to be done right. Individuals have to do their own tasks well, yet everything must be coordinated. It is the job of the captain—the general manager—to get his or her crew to think and act in a coordinated way: to understand goals and the policies designed to get the ship to those goals, as well as the changes that may be necessary to make at a moment's notice if circumstances change. The ship's captain must help sail the ship through dangerous waters, and must always calculate the risk of any action. Setting sail doesn't help if one doesn't know where the ship is going. Knowing the destination with no plan on how to get there is little better. Even getting to the destination is not enough if the passage has caused great damage to the ship and high casualties among the crew, making another voyage impossible.

When the ship is small, the captain may have little or no crew, and of necessity will be personally involved in all aspects of sailing the ship. As the ship he or she skippers becomes larger, the captain must hire more and more crew to carry out individual tasks. He or she must step back from the nitty-gritty and take more of a management role if the ship is to sail at maximum efficiency. Some will find this transition an easy one, others will find it less suited to their skills and personal styles. It is necessary for a captain to have had some experience with the tasks that must be overseen, either as a sailor for another captain or as captain of a small vessel, which involved undertaking all the various tasks required to sail the craft.

Lee Iacocca, chairman of the Chrysler Corporation, is a good example of a successful modern-day industrial captain. He assumed the helm of a nearly bankrupt, rudderless, sinking corporation. But he had a vision of Chrysler's future, and was able to use that vision to put into place the policies necessary to steady Chrysler and move it slowly but surely toward success. Part of this was a matter of changing the crew, but much of it was adapting the corporate ship to the modern world and getting Chrysler's crew to think about the race as it must be run today, not as it had been successfully run for the previous twenty years. The changes included redesigning front-wheel-drive cars, introducing aggressive marketing programs, lowering labor costs, improving the quality of workmanship, and securing huge government-backed loans. Iacocca proved himself a master at making the large corporate ship sail.

Other corporate captains are more at home in smaller, lighter craft. The computer software industry is littered with successful small companies and their captains who have found growing difficult and often painful. Many of these entrepreneurs have found that the yacht is not nearly as much fun to sail as the sunfish—communicating how, when, and why so that others can steer the corporate ship is not as satisfying to these captains as sailing by themselves, or with the help of a small trusted crew. Many of these entrepreneurs have sold their companies or given up their day-to-day management to "professional managers" in order to go out and seek other challenges—often building and sailing another small corporate ship.

The HBS Business Policy course is concerned with the actions and responsibilities associated with setting the direction and giving the orders for all areas of the ship—or business—in order to increase the odds of a smooth passage and a timely arrival at the desired destination.

THE NEED FOR LEADERSHIP AND VISION

The "complete" general manager as seen by HBS is an organizational leader, a leader of people, and a corporate visionary. Of course, everyone is stronger in one area than another, and confident managers try to surround themselves with other top managers who complement their strengths and weaknesses.

The common view is that an *organizational leader* does a specific job well and delegates to others the jobs the leader is less qualified to do. This person takes responsibility for results, and often leaves the getting there to others. This person often tries to build a strong organization to run the business after he or she has left. IBM stresses the need for strong organizational leadership skills to progress within its highly structured and highly successful corporate environment.

Exercising *personal leadership* involves using judgment where policies are not clear-cut and possibly can't be. The leader motivates others by example, creating an atmosphere in which people like to work and setting standards for performance and behavior, often touching the lives of staff members in a significant way. Ted Turner would be considered a person who succeeds by personal leadership. His often brassy style permeates his businesses, as does his personal vision.

Corporate visionaries go beyond running the business. They look at the society in which their business operates and into the future of that society in order to give the business direction and purpose. Ray Kroc gazed into the future and saw a food service industry dominated by fast-food purveyors. Today, over 15,000 McDonald's around the world attest to the accuracy of his vision. Henry Ford envisioned a world that rode on wheels without horses in front of them. Edward N. Ney looked into the future of the advertising business and saw global firms capable of providing any marketing communications service a client could ever need. Today his firm, Young and Rubicam, Inc., is number one in worldwide billings and considered the model to follow by much of the industry.

No less visionary is the auto assembly-line manager who allows only the highest quality finished automobiles to leave his assembly area because he firmly believes that quality is Job One (to use a catchy Ford marketing term) for success in today's marketplace.

Clearly, the job of the general manager as taught at Harvard through its Business Policy case studies is a demanding and diverse one. It entails far more than crunching numbers and pushing paper. Perhaps it is this larger perspective on general management that has enabled so many Harvard graduates to progress to the top in the corporate world. Whether it is or not, the Business Policy course, which is at the core of the

HBS program, is the vehicle for communicating this concept of the general manager's role, and for instructing prospective general managers in the analytic techniques necessary to perform that role successfully.

CORPORATE STRATEGIES, GOALS, AND POLICIES

Every company seeks continually to better its business. But toward what ultimate goal is it headed in pursuit of a brighter future? That corporate goal, and the strategy for getting there, must be stated—and, over time, reevaluated, revised, and restated—rather than assumed to be implicit, if a company is to be managed effectively and run smoothly. There must be an agreed-upon set of overall decisions about the company's direction, against which all other decisions at all levels of the company can be measured.

As one school of thought has it, a company must be able to define in one sentence what business it's in. Railroad companies that saw themselves only in the railroad business shortly after World War II lost out to railroad companies that saw themselves in the transportation business and diversified accordingly. Today, newspaper publishing companies are asking themselves if they are in the newspaper business, the print communications business, or the communications business. Industry executives must forecast which strategy will pan out. Market dynamics will ultimately determine the winners and losers.

Corporate strategy is the overall plan a company designs to make its way in the business world. Rather than a decision made at a specific time, corporate strategy is a series of decisions made on an ongoing basis. These strategy decisions ultimately determine what businesses a company is in and how it will compete; the kind of organization it will set up and the kind of people it will try to attract; as well as the commitments it will make to various stakeholders in the company, including employees, stockholders, customers, suppliers, and the community at large.

If a company is in many different businesses, it will have a number of business strategies that should all support the overall corporate strategy.

Every company's strategy is unique, somewhat like a human fingerprint. Although corporate strategies may look similar, when examined closely they have marked differences.

Consider the differences between IBM and Digital Equipment Corporation in the computer world, McDonald's and Burger King in fast food, Ford and Chrysler on the nations highways, Delta and Eastern in the friendly skies, and Coke and Pepsi just about everywhere. Senior management must make sure that a company's strategy is clearly defined and that it is appropriate, given the company's resources and its competitive environment.

After a corporate strategy and set of overall goals is determined, policies must be instituted for conducting business and reaching the goals. Corporate strategy basically answers the question, What must this company do to be viable in the future? Business policies respond to the questions that are generated when the first question is answered, namely: Now that the company has decided what business it is in, how should the company and product lines be structured so that they are competitive and successful? These policies must be well defined and well communicated at all levels of the organization.

One unique illustration of an especially powerful business policy is provided by the nation of Japan, where due to the cooperative relationship between the private and public sectors, employees, management, suppliers, and even the government all share a clear understanding of the direction of a particular business and work toward common goals. It is almost as if the entire country—Japan Inc.—has been molded into a consortium of well-run businesses with strong business policies designed to help compete effectively in world markets.

Government and industrial leaders set the long-term direction and then all segments of the public and private sectors fall into line with programs designed to accomplish Japan Inc.'s goals.

In the United States, of course, the basic business and governmental relationships are far different. However, many American companies have clear, well-defined and well-communicated business strategies. In fact, the companies cited in Thomas J. Peters and Robert H. Waterman, Jr.'s, best seller, *In Search of Excellence*, are examples of companies whose success is due, in important part, to their highly effective business policies. Procter & Gamble, IBM, McDonald's, 3M, Delta Airlines, Maytag, and Marriott are examples of companies that know where they are going and work hard to put in place consistent policies that ensure coordinated movement in the desired direction from all segments of their companies. Compare these companies with others in a random sample and one realizes how unusual and impressive an achievement business policy is in any business, and particularly in one of considerable size.

How often in our own companies do we see one manager hell-bent on attaining growth while another in the same department seeks slower growth and higher profits? When was the last interdepartmental skirmish, with one department emphasizing improved quality and another trying to find ways to slash costs and speed up delivery times? More often than not, nobody in a company knows where it is going, let alone everybody. The Business Policy course at HBS teaches that setting strong overall direction—with supporting policies put into play—is possibly the single most important step in running a continually successful business.

ANALYZING AND IMPLEMENTING CORPORATE STRATEGY

As business people, we all make countless decisions, large and small, each day. Many decisions we make almost unconsciously. Others we ponder. Which problems to work on? Which

data to analyze? Which types of analysis to do? Which recommendations to make? Whom to communicate with? What
to say? When to fight and when to give in at the first sign of
resistance?

Harvard stresses the value of having in mind decision-making
models for use in the process of case analysis. This is a way
of helping students identify all of the different issues that must
be analyzed and also understand how the various analytic
components are interrelated. Experienced managers often find
the use of models unnecessary. But even for seasoned veterans,
studying models can help identify areas requiring clearly set
policies, the articulation of which might otherwise be overlooked.

STEP ONE: ANALYSIS OF FIXED ELEMENTS

The first step in developing a strong business-policy analysis
is to identify and analyze the "immovable object" elements in
the environment in which a decision is being made—the
elements over which one has no control. These are called *fixed
elements*. These elements, which cannot be manipulated by
management, form the constraints within which management
must operate.

A number of areas must be examined to create this model,
and a number of questions must be answered.

First, the competitive environment must be assessed. Companies must determine what business they are in and who the
main competitors are.

For example, in today's world of diversified communications, management of a newspaper must ask itself more questions than it did thirty years ago when all it needed to ask was,
How can we do better than our crosstown rival? Today, it must
get down to basics and ask itself whether it is competing with
other newspapers and if so, which ones? What are the effects
of the *New York Times* and *Wall Street Journal*, two national
newspapers, on its readership? Is *USA Today* cutting into the
readership? Are old readers being lured by suburban news-

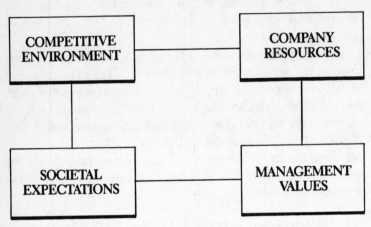

FIGURE 1-1. Fixed Element Analysis Model

newspapers that give more coverage of news in their towns than the old city metro? Is the newspaper competing with magazines, television, and radio? And must the newspaper compete as an entertainment medium and as a news-and-information medium?

Other questions about the competitive environment must be asked. Who are the key competitors? What are their goals, strengths, and weaknesses? How can this company compete against them and how is it vulnerable?

Another important series of questions relates to the issues of what barriers exist to keep other companies from coming in and stealing business. These are called *barriers to entry* into a market, and can include—

- *Product Differentiation.* Does the company have a unique product that competitors will find hard to copy, like a Mercedes automobile or a Sony television?
- *Patents.* Does the company hold any special patents or other protections (copyrights, trademarks, etc.) that could

legally protect it from imitators? A patentable drug, for instance, is legally free from competition from an identical chemical component for eighteen years from the time the patent is granted.

- *Economies of Scale.* Can the company gain economic advantage over competitors by becoming larger, producing more, and lowering per-unit costs in comparison to those of competitors?

    In the brewing business, Budweiser beer has created enormous economies of scale. The brand is far and away America's number one beer. As its brewing and distribution costs-per-unit decline, it gains more and more after-cost revenue to advertise and promote itself. This added product visibility has helped Budweiser to pull even further ahead of competitors in sales, which allows it to effect even greater economies of scale.

    A clear result of the barrier to entry in the brewing business caused by economies of scale is the steady decline of smaller local and regional breweries to the point where the top six U.S. brewers now account for over 90 percent of sales in the U.S. beer market.

- *Capital Requirements.* What are the start-up or expansion costs, and will they restrict business competition?

- *Access to Distribution.* Is access to distribution limited, and can those who have good distribution insulate themselves from competitive attack?

- *Customer Loyalty.* Is customer loyalty strong in this product group? Customer loyalty is quite different from product to product. Where customer loyalty is strong it is difficult for competitors to enter and succeed in the market. Often, these new competitors must seek to expand the base of the market to create a niche for themselves.

    Smokers seldom switch from Marlboros to a new cigarette just to try something different, nor does price usually affect cigarette smokers' choice of brand. On the other hand, drinkers of Becks, Heineken, Molson Golden and other imported beers generally don't hesitate to try new products and products that are on sale. They often don't switch completely to the new product, but their loyalty to a particular brand is not fierce.

- *Government Regulation.* Can government regulation be used to hinder competition in a market or does less regulation allow other market forces enumerated above to work against competition? For years, government regulation insulated the airline industry from excess competition, ensuring healthy profits for all. Today, only the fittest carriers prosper.

After analyzing the competition, carefully assess your own company resources. What are the company's major strengths in relation to its competitors—product quality? lower cost? marketing clout? greater financial resources? What are its major weaknesses—product quality? distribution? sales force? The best corporate strategies are those that draw upon a company's strengths while minimizing its weaknesses.

Third, society's expectations for the enterprise must be analyzed. Does society expect the firm to reap huge profits? Pay a lot in taxes? Provide jobs? Invest locally? What will anger society? How important is public opinion, especially bad public opinion? Will it affect company performance?

If the public gets angry at the Defense Department's strongest supplier of submarines, that company will probably still prosper. But if the local tavern owner consistently serves minors or has bands that are too loud for the neighborhood, he may soon be out of business.

Management values is another important area that needs analysis. In what direction will the values of its management lead a company? What directions will they prohibit? Does management most value growth and profits or is a stable, livable work environment more important? Is performance most valued or honesty and loyalty to the company?

This last fixed element is a very important one to think through carefully in setting business policy. HBS stresses it in many different ways. Everyone has a personal value system.

Companies are made up of many people and the strongest companies have value systems that accurately reflect the values of senior managers.

IBM and Apple are both very successful players in computers but they have strikingly different value systems. "Big Blue" values conformity to its many well-thought-out systems all the way down to its strict, though unwritten, dress code. This conformity has been a part of the company's value system since the time of its earliest managers and is based, in part at least, on the notion that all should outwardly appear to be pushing for the corporate good. Apple, on the other hand, would have had a riot on its hands if Steve Jobs had told everyone they had to wear suspenders and bow ties, and he would have been forced out of the company earlier and for different reasons than he was. Each company's policies have been designed to be effective given its own unique set of fixed values.

One additional analytical step is to look beyond the profits that a business or group of competitors is earning today and try to predict how profitable the future will be for all. A strong aid in this area, the Five Forces model, is explained fully in *Competitive Strategies*, a book used extensively at HBS and written by Michael E. Porter, one of the school's highly respected professors.

In simple terms, Professor Porter's model argues that long-term profitability will be low if the level of competition and rivalry in a business is intense. The long-term intensity of rivalry in any industry can be predicted by studying four factors.

First, study the number of potential entrants into a category. If the number of potential entrants into the marketplace is high, the level of rivalry will rise and profits will be distributed among more and more competitors. This is where the barriers to entry become important. If the barriers are numerous and high, as they are in the brewing industry, few new competitors will be able to join the party even though profits may be high. The cost of new plants and heavy advertising will be prohibitive. But if the barriers are low, as they are in the personal computer software industry (although they are getting higher all the time), hundreds of competitors can appear quickly wherever profits seem high. The result: Profits quickly disappear and many firms go out of business.

Second, look ahead and see if potential substitutes exist for your product or business. If they do, at a certain time down the road they could begin competing in your arena and dramatically raise the level of rivalry. In the mid-1970s, it looked like oil prices and profits might rise forever. But as oil became rapidly more expensive, many new energy competitors appeared. Coal became competitive again and nuclear power once again became a viable option. Solar water heaters and, where feasible, heating systems sprang up. Home owners even found burning wood became worth the effort again. Rather quickly these substitutes increased the rivalry for energy dollars, and flattened both demand and price trends within the oil industry.

Third, consider the power of suppliers in an industry. A low level of that power tends to increase the level of rivalry, allowing more suppliers to gain contracts, but decreasing their chances for high profits. In the oil situation cited, as prices rose, more competitors entered the market and suppliers lost power. Auto companies can buy their standard parts from many domestic or foreign suppliers. This decreases suppliers' power. If you want to do business with GM, you probably do it on GM's terms.

But it may be possible, with a clever business strategy and resourceful marketing, to build a position of strength as a supplier, outdistancing competitors and thereby producing the opportunity for high profits.

NutraSweet is a perfect example. While many companies could supply sugar substitute products to Coke, Pepsi, 7-Up and other soft drinks, the G.D. Searle Company, makers of NutraSweet, had the foresight to go out and build consumer demand for its brand name. As a result, every food and beverage manufacturer wants the NutraSweet brand in its product. Searle has thus put itself in a powerful position as a supplier and so stands to reap huge profits.

Last, consider the power of buyers in an industry. When the power of buyers is high, rivalry for their purchase will rise and profit margins will normally sink. If you want to sell basic whitewall tires to car manufacturers, you don't have too many buyers to choose from. You had better have a superior, differentiated product, or resign yourself to keeping a very low price and low profit margin.

STEP TWO: CONTROLLABLE ELEMENT ANALYSIS

Given the constraints placed on a company and outlined in the fixed elements analysis, management must then work with the many variables over which it does have control to construct its business policy. These controllable elements must be analyzed in order to create the best possible corporate strategy for a particular company, given its unique position in the marketplace.

Marketing policies must be analyzed. What should the company produce? How should those products be positioned? How should they be priced? What is the best way to distribute those products? How should the product be advertised and promoted?

Manufacturing policies need careful attention. What type of manufacturing process is best to produce the type and quantity of products the company desires? Where should manufacturing and distribution facilities be located? Should the company manufacture continually or seasonally? What role will new technologies play in operations?

Integrated financial policies must be developed. What performance goals does the company want to set in terms of profits, operating margins, and return on capital? Will the company's funds come from operations, debt, or equity? How much ownership will management retain? How much will employees own? How much will the public own?

Research and development policies must also be set. What percentage of sales will be plowed back into R&D? Will R&D efforts be long-term in nature or more short-term/application-oriented? Will R&D be done for the whole company at the

FIGURE 1-2. Controllable Element Analysis Model

corporate level or will it be done within each division? Who will manage R&D operations? Are R&D joint ventures in the firm's best interest?

Human resources policies are also critical. What type of people will the company seek to employ? How will employees be compensated? Will salaries be high or low? Will the compensation be all salary or less salary and greater opportunities for bonuses?

Issues of corporate structure must be investigated. How will the company be structured to maximize success in the marketplace?

THE BUSINESS POLICY RECOMMENDATION

HBS students go through this type of analysis for each BP case, usually twenty-five to forty pages in length, using all the written data given them as well as their own experience and judgment. Since sleep is necessary to sustain life even at Harvard Business

School, students quickly learn that it is critical to identify and concentrate on the most important aspects of the analysis—which will vary depending on the case—while moving briskly through less important areas.

Once the analysis is completed, students are asked to formulate a recommended short- and long-term strategic plan for the company in question, including a full set of integrated policies in the areas of marketing, production, finance, and human resources.

Again, a number of questions must be asked and answered; the answer to each question will often raise another series of questions.

HBS students gradually learn that a strong BP presentation, whether it is a class opening, a final exam write-up, a presentation to a company's strategic planning committee, or a recommendation to one's boss, should include the following:

- A summary of critical pieces of analysis upon which the recommendation rests
- An overall statement of corporate goals, both short- and long-term
- A clear summary of the business(es) the company is in today and those it wants to be in in the future
- A description of how the company sees itself positioned in those businesses and how it plans to differentiate itself from key competitors now and in the future
- An identification of key success factors, such as product quality, financial strengths, and distribution channels, which must be monitored to accomplish the company's identified goals
- An outline of key functional policies, such as marketing, finance, and human resources, that must be carefully integrated to assure achievement of the key success factors
- Identification of the barriers that could prevent achievement of strategic goals, and description of contingency plans should those barriers arise.

Readers are probably asking, Read the case and do that analysis in two to four hours? Harvard's answer is yes. Students need to prepare two or three cases each day. And, when semester exams come around, they are four hours. So students must work toward getting their analysis done fast as well as done well.

CLASS DISCUSSION OF A BP CASE

An international pharmaceuticals company has an enormous profit margin, with a very high percentage of its total profits from selling high-quality infant formula in developing countries. However, fairly strong scientific as well as moral arguments are being raised to the effect that packaged formula should be used only by mothers who are incapable of breast feeding because of the formula's high cost and lower nutritional value. Bottle feeding makes babies more susceptible to disease and probably leads to heightened infant mortality.

One country is on the verge of passing tough, restrictive legislation, but many others are only beginning to discuss the issue.

As the president of the company whose stock is selling for more than twenty times the forecasted earnings, what should BP recommendation be?

The class Humanists kick off the discussion by arguing that it is immoral to encourage penniless third-world mothers to spend money and endanger their kids' health for profits. They argue that the firm has no choice but to stop marketing in developing countries immediately.

A Quantitative Analysis Jock calculates total profits from the formula sales, what percentage of the company's profits are made by formula sales, its margins, what the chances are of making that kind of money in any other business and concludes:

- The business is a gold mine.
- The company has a responsibility to its shareholders to maximize profits in any legal manner possible.

- Image advertising, "buying" recommendations from physicians, and other ways to stem the bad publicity could work to stall regulatory efforts and keep the profits flowing.

The Humanists and a few Synthesizers counter that what is morally wrong can never lead to good long-term profits, and that the company will be fighting a long, drawn-out holding action against bad publicity and will inevitably lose. Funds will be committed that could be spent more productively on production, new products, modernization, and better employee incentives.

The Political Animals are laying low on this one, unable to see any way to stake out a winning position in this messy argument. Class opinions vary widely on this issue and change dramatically as one argument seems to hold sway, only to be knocked down by another.

One of the class iconoclasts will eloquently and graphically point out that he or she has traveled in many of these countries, that the native people are terribly poor and often spend all their available cash on infant formula because they have a naive faith in western products, which makes the situation all the more terrible. Nature's method has worked for thousands of years, this person says, so why should we change it merely for the sake of our profits?

The class blackboards are by now covered with information on what businesses the company is in, how much money is at stake for the company, how much money stockholders might lose if sales were curtailed, what options the company has to increase sales in other areas and to decrease sales in this area, as well as a myriad of other information.

The Skydeckers, who have seemingly been asleep in their skydeck seats for the first eighty-five minutes of this ninety-minute class, now awake, preen themselves and survey the scene like hawks on a perch. The complicated discussion is slowly building toward a consensus as the class winds down. Suddenly a hand shoots up from the back row, and the startled professor calls on the Skydecker, who spends the last few moments of the class, in a relaxed fashion, arguing that long-term profits can be sustained only if products fill a real need and are seen as positive aspects of people's lives. There is an obvious need for the company to rethink its hard-sell marketing approaches for its long-term good. It needs to find a way to do this in a gradual way in order to maximize profits during the transition and minimize guilt and negative publicity. Quoting John D. Rockefeller or Lee Iacocca, in a resounding conclusion on corporate responsibility, the Skydecker will leave the class speechless, and exit one minute before the end of the session, the better to claim a prime tanning spot on the main lawn in front of Baker Library.

Debate will rage on even after the class has ended and many students have left. Some students will be truly upset by the seeming insensitivity of certain classmates, some of whom will have enjoyed playing the devil's advocate. Others will be appalled that certain Humanists might really turn their backs on such enormous profits being earned in a perfectly legal fashion by a high-quality product.

The only thing everyone will have agreed upon is that no single right answer was identified although the debate made it very clear what the stakes were, what key issues existed, and what the most realistic strategic and policy options were.

Another victory for the HBS method.

BACK TO REALITY

We should add two notes of caution on considering and formulating a corporate strategy.

First, setting corporate strategy and policies is not worth much unless they are clearly communicated and implemented, and result in the desired level of corporate performance. Corporate strategy is only one element, albeit a very important one, in business success. If corporate performance doesn't measure up to expectations, management must be careful to identify the problems before making changes. Lower-than-expected results could be caused by a miscalculation of variables when making strategy, or by a change in prospects for the business, or possibly by a change in business conditions for the entire economy.

A second caution: Don't expect corporate strategy and policies to be perfect in the first design. Optimal strategies and policies evolve over time, as the company grows and matures, and as the managers who run the company experiment with and fine-tune their operation. Companies must work hard to get good ongoing corporate strategy assessment, whether it be on a monthly, weekly, or daily basis. The process is difficult to maintain, but the result—a current, accurate, sound strategy—is extremely important to a company; which, of course, cannot be said of a business plan that is no longer pertinent to the company or the environment in which it operates.

Even with these cautions, the HBS message is clear: The development of the strongest possible business policy is, for any company, one of its general manager's most difficult yet highest priority responsibilities.

BUSINESS POLICY CHECKLIST

To say that there is no single recipe for building a successful corporate strategy is to deal in understatement. There are, however, a number of basic ingredients that a company needs to incorporate into its strategy. It is in the proportioning of those ingredients—making up the strategic mix—that managers can outline a distinctive profile for their company and, in doing so, at least partially determine its ultimate success.

When checking to see if a company has an effective business policy, the following brief checklist of questions can provide a helpful start.

1. Can the company's overall corporate strategy and market position be summarized in two or three sentences?
2. Given a brief analysis of the company, the competition, and the industry as a whole, does the current corporate strategy seem to be optimal in light of the company's

strengths and weaknesses and its competitive environment?

3. Does the current corporate strategy effectively anticipate possible near-term and long-term changes in the marketplace?

4. Has the corporate strategy been effectively communicated to all levels of personnel in the company? Are the majority of employees in agreement with the company's long-term goals and objectives?

5. Have policies been put in place within the various functional areas of the company—marketing, sales, finance, human resources—so that employees have guidelines and incentives that make their long-term interest consistent with the long-term interest of the company?

6. Does the company have people with the necessary vision developing and implementing corporate strategy and business policies on an ongoing basis?

2

ORGANIZATIONAL BEHAVIOR

It is one thing to be able to design elegant business policy strategies. It is a totally different matter to translate brilliant strategic thinking into corporate action.

Management experts have noted that strong companies that are able to remain strong have the capacity to implement change successfully when necessary. The Organizational Behavior class at HBS, known as OB, deals with issues that help students understand what is perhaps the critical element of implementing business strategies: getting people to act in a manner that yields desired results.

CASE: THE AUTO INDUSTRY

Let's consider some of the current problems of the U.S. auto industry.

How many times over the past ten years have we lamented

that Japanese cars cost $1,500 to $2,000 less than U.S.-produced autos, which are of lesser quality. All this, we are told, because of the low wages and superior work habits of the Japanese labor force; and because of the innovative production techniques and hundreds of millions of dollars' worth of sophisticated robots at work in Japan's ultra-modern factories, thanks to the support of government funds.

Poor Detroit. How can union-saddled GM, Ford, and Chrysler possibly compete? Especially with the enormous bonuses these companies have paid their top executives since the early 1980s. Building autos in the United States seemingly puts American manufacturers at a terrible disadvantage.

When Volkswagen opened a plant in Pennsylvania and consumers started reporting significant reliability problems with VW Rabbits, complaints about manufacturing in the United States seemed substantiated.

Then Honda began building four-door Accords in Ohio and Nissan light trucks started rolling off assembly lines in Tennessee, with very interesting results. Careful analysis has shown that these U.S.-built products are equal to and in some cases superior to those built in Japan, with costs low enough to make production in the United States viable and profitable.

Their success raises many interesting issues. American workers are employed at both the Honda and the Nissan plants. Even much of the management is American. And neither plant uses significantly more robot technology than Detroit uses. Even the basic supply and production methods employed are similar to those of GM, Ford, and Chrysler. What is the secret to success for Honda's and Nissan's U.S. operations?

Many experts believe that it is rooted in their sensitive organizational behavior management policies. Nissan and Honda workers are made to feel that they are important, that they have a say in how things are done, that their skill and attention to product quality is the key to their company's success, and that if the company prospers, everyone will share the profits. As a result, workers often work for less cash compensation;

they work harder, work better and give the company back great value for its labor dollar.

Careful attention to organizational behavior issues—such as company culture, worker involvement in company decision-making, worker job satisfaction, profit sharing and clear communication of company goals—is helping Honda and Nissan translate their business policies into highly effective corporate performance.

THE HBS CLASS

Through thirty-five case analyses, the HBS Organizational Behavior course stresses that business enterprises are made up of human beings and that business managers can only be successful if they are keenly aware of their employees' feelings, needs, and motivations. The ultimate objective of the OB course is to improve the ability of prospective managers to manage people; to enable these managers to meet their short- and long-term objectives, as well as the objectives of the people they manage. Students are taught how to manage human and corporate dynamics in order to create the likelihood of a positive outcome in any situation. They become aware of the potential impact of corporate structure, corporate culture, and office politics on their plans.

The purpose of HBS's OB course is not to make students organizational behavior experts, psychologists, or organizational design specialists, but to heighten their awareness and understanding of—

1. The organization as a system of many interactive dynamic factors, which managers can modify when appropriate
2. The kinds of factors one should take into consideration when contemplating trying to make changes within an organization
3. The need for managers to assess carefully those factors

over which they have direct control, partial control, or
no control in any given situation

4. The need for managers to assess carefully every situation
    and formulate a well-thought-out plan for asking people
    to take a given action or make a behavioral change.

The OB course is divided into two major parts.

The first part introduces students to some of the management problems that arise when working with people. The course deals with problems encountered in managing oneself, one-to-one relationships, small groups, and large groups. Through readings on current behavioral theory and discussion of case studies, and through role-playing and viewing and analyzing films, students improve their judgment in dealing with complex problems that involve managing people. The second part of the course builds on the first and on the Human Resource Management course. It addresses how to maintain an effective organization given continual internal and external change. Through case studies and a mock consulting project, students learn how to analyze, diagnose, and manage the dynamic interrelationship involving the business environment, corporate goals and strategies, the organizational design of the corporation, its operating systems, the types of people who work in the organization, their jobs, and the culture of the company.

While Business Policy is particularly enjoyed by Synthesizers, OB is the sinecure of Humanists and Eccentrics. Of course, humanists by nature tend to empathize with people and their feelings. Eccentrics, for their part, tend to bring a street savvy to the table that enables them to foresee complicated human dynamics and "office politics" for the important issues that they are.

OB is often perceived as a "gut" course—until the midterm rolls around, when low passes and unsatisfactory grades are received by 10 to 20 percent of the students in each section, many of whom find themselves doing very well in the more quantitative courses. Though the OB course is often thought of as soft or mushy, the concepts involved are probably the most often needed in business. In many cases business failures and ineffective job performance are due to OB problems rather than to a lack of strategy or intellect.

The major reason this course is so difficult for many people is also the reason why general managers who manage people sensitively and who are consistently successful in achieving expected results are paid very well:

1. There are a multitude of organizational behavior factors to consider and trace at any point, and these dynamics are always shifting, so that if a decision is made but not acted on rapidly the decision may need to be rethought.
2. There is no single proper way to do things. Personal judgment and personal style are critical elements. Perceptiveness, imagination, and flexibility are hallmarks of managers with a good feel for OB issues. Being able to anticipate and manage OB issues is one of the crucial things that separates an effective manager from a mere administrator.

Judgment is the key, and it is a skill HBS tries to develop in its students through the case-study method. Although gut feeling is an important factor in judgment, the more complex the situation, the more chancy it is for a manager to be guided solely by instinct. Our aim in this chapter is to introduce many of the concepts of the OB course that are the conceptual building blocks that enable one to exercise good judgment.

We'll do this, just a few pages ahead, through the use of a brief case study from the banking industry. We were surprised to find at HBS that one could go through an entire OB course apparently comprehending the theory, then become totally confused trying to put that theory into practice in a case study. Rather than try to lay out all the OB theory in twenty-five pages, we felt it better to look at a case study and try to illustrate some of the theoretical highlights along the way.

THE OB DECISION-MAKERS

Many people believe that the primary responsibility for dealing with OB and human relations problems should fall to human resource managers and personnel managers.

This could not be further from the truth. Nissan and Honda, IBM and McDonald's are not being managed by their personnel departments.

HBS teaches that all of us, regardless of our status in the organization, must be aware of OB problems and able to solve them. OB decisions are made at all levels of the organization— by managers, supervisors, group leaders, and non-management employees. All members of the organization are trying to get things done, for themselves as well as for the company.

Each person has to relate to peers, bosses, and perhaps subordinates, as well as to customers, suppliers, competitors, and others. Although we will focus primarily on problems a manager would be called on to solve, keep in mind that all of the same notions of human dynamics apply to situations you might find yourself in as an individual, in both your professional and personal life.

In the OB cases studied at HBS, students are asked to put themselves in a variety of situations, including the position of—

- CEO of a small but rapidly growing insurance company who is trying to decide whether to reorganize his company and if so in what way
- A newly assigned prison warden asked to reform a prison's savage conditions in the face of a strongly entrenched prison culture
- A general foreman required to turn around a production department in which output and quality are poor and costs are skyrocketing
- Director of Johnson Space Center in Houston, faced with

a possible strike by Skylab 3 astronauts who were feeling ill and overworked.

OB DECISIONS AND THEIR IMPORTANCE

The heart of organizational behavior is managing a situation toward an ultimate goal.

A manager is called on to make a decision because something is not working the way it should. Or, the leaders of an organization decide to introduce a change into the business. They must figure out a way to do it without disruption. Or a manager may want to move to a new division and must orchestrate the situation carefully to facilitate the transfer.

HBS students learn that when managing an OB situation, one must try to ally each worker's interests with those of the company or those of the decision-maker so that when people work to serve their self-interest, they serve the overall interest as well.

It is up to a manager to put in place formal organizational structures and operating systems, and to use the culture and office politics to advantage in order to meet the corporate goals and the manager's personal goals. By determining structural elements and establishing an interpersonal style, the manager communicates goals to the employees. This communication, through words and actions, must be clear and consistent, so that workers understand the goals of the corporation and how they can contribute—and be rewarded.

The importance of OB decision-making cannot be overestimated. At Honda and Nissan, programs have been put in place to help individual workers meet a number of their personal goals. Among these are bettering individual career potential and position, improving job skills, gaining a perception of personal influence within the company, feeling a stronger sense of belonging to a peer and corporate group, and simply enjoying their jobs.

Honda and Nissan also attain a number of corporate goals with their organizational behavior programs. Among these are lowering wage rates while attracting higher quality employees; gaining higher productivity, lower turnover, and better employee morale; and achieving greater creativity and flexibility on the assembly line.

THE BANKING INDUSTRY
1975–1985

The banking industry has recently undergone significant changes, and faced major OB issues at both the structural and personal levels.

Let's look at the structural changes the industry has gone through, then some of the interpersonal issues that management has had to deal with to make those structural changes work.

First, a word about corporate structure.

If we were to start a company from scratch, or to consider wholesale redesigning of an existing company, the first questions we should ask are, What should the corporate structure, or organizational design, look like? How many employees do we need? What job functions make sense? Who should report to whom?

The organizational design determines what the reporting relationships are within the company. One of the major objectives in designing an organization should be to enable the company to deliver its product or service to its customers most effectively and efficiently given its strategic goals and desired market position. A well-designed corporate structure also enables management to minimize duplication of work; to attain maximum flexibility; and to maximize communication throughout the organization.

Although on paper it may seem easy to design an effective organization, in reality there are many problems associated with design, including personality conflicts that may make it difficult to establish certain reporting relationships; ingrained ways of operating that make it difficult to introduce new systems and technologies; or physical limitations such as space constraints in existing company quarters that may make the cost of reorganization prohibitive.

We have three basic theoretical options for our corporate structure design: a functional design, a divisional design, or a matrix design. Many companies choose a variation on one of these themes. There are inherent strengths and weaknesses in each design.

Option 1: Functional Design

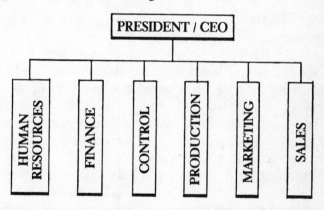

FIGURE 2–1. Functional Organizational Structure

The functional design tends to be used in a company operating in a fairly stable market with a single product or limited product line in which there are only infrequent product changes. This type of design encourages centralized decision-making.

Positive aspects of the functional design include specialization of tasks, which reduces territorial battles and duplication of efforts; development of functional experts, which can be satisfying for many professionals; and lower overhead due to the economies of scale within each function.

Weaknesses of this corporate structure include narrow functional vision, which makes it difficult to meet rapidly changing customer needs; difficulty in getting one group to understand the goals and needs of other groups; poor coordination across functional lines; and difficulty in developing general management talent within management ranks because everyone tends to specialize.

Option 2: Divisional Design

A company that has a divisional design could be split along many different lines. Companies such as Procter & Gamble split themselves along product lines. Others—banks being a good example—split themselves along the lines of customer profile. Still others, like McDonald's, split themselves into geographic regions.

This design tends to be used in a company with a more complicated product line and/or distribution network, which demands that the company is market driven and that decisions are made in a decentralized fashion. In this model, decisions can be made at the lowest possible organizational level for faster turnaround than is possible in a centralized company.

Among the positive aspects of divisional design are that it enables decisions to be made relatively quickly and that it facilitates the development of general management talent. Perhaps the most important aspect of this structure is that the priority becomes gleaning expertise from all functions in order to best meet product, customer, geographic, and distribution needs. In addition, the natural competition between divisions can be used to motivate employees.

Problems inherent in this design are that it may increase overhead and duplicate use of resources; and divisional competition produces stress on managers.

Option 3: Matrix Design

Two types of companies that often use the matrix design are consulting firms and advertising agencies. In these firms there are project managers who are responsible for seeing that each project is completed to specifications in a timely manner. The project manager coordinates the talent required to accomplish each project, drawing on individuals throughout the company

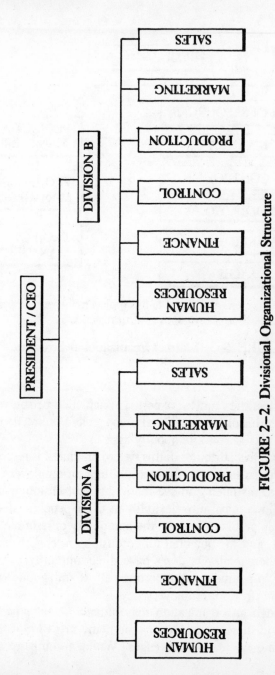

FIGURE 2–2. Divisional Organizational Structure

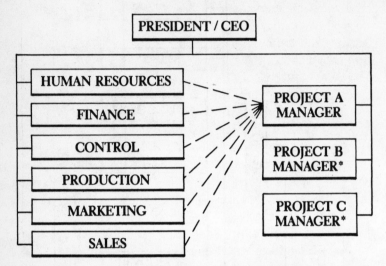

*Functional experts also report to this project manager on a project-by-project basis as shown above with Project A.

FIGURE 2–3. Matrix Organizational Structure

who possess the required expertise. Each such person reports directly to his or her functional manager and indirectly to the project manager on a temporary basis.

The positive attributes of this system are that it is responsive to specific customer needs; it is fulfilling for employees, who change teams often and see many different customer needs; and it allows maximum flexibility in using people's talents.

Possible problems include the complexity of resource management, and the potential for confusion or conflict that can occur when managers don't have direct authority over employees. In addition, the reporting path is ambiguous, which can cause stress for employees.

Although an organization may initially be set up to look like one of these models, over time many structures will tend to become unclear at the edges. When a company asks a manager, a management team or a consultant to restructure the company, it may be asking for an alternative organizational design, or it may be asking that individual or group just to tinker with the current design and tighten the existing structure. Sometimes a number of structures must be tried before one works effectively.

In the banking industry, because of the deregulation of both products and geographic boundaries since the early 1980s, the context in which individual banks do business has changed dramatically. Rapid advances in technology, as well as increased competition in banking and financial services, have caused banks to change their strategy for achieving both profits and growth.

Margins on deposits and loans declined due to competition. No longer would simply acquiring a volume of deposits or loans increase profits. Many new loans were made in an attempt to maximize loan balances because lower-quality loans were going bad. Loan losses soared. Many banks realized— some, like Continental Illinois, not early enough—that to compete profitably and to stay out of bankruptcy, they were going to have to secure a position in profitable niches of the financial services industry. No longer could all banks try to be everything to everyone. They had to concentrate on overall profits, not simply on asset/loan growth.

These changes led many banks to conclude from a business policy point of view that they had to become less centralized, more customer driven, and more closely attuned with the marketplace. Profitable market niches had to be identified and then specialized groups within the bank had to be developed to sell to and service those high-profit customers.

As a result, since the early 1980s, many commercial banks have reorganized, moving from a functional structure to a divisional system organized around specific customer profiles and needs. In many of these banks, each division is headed by a general manager who directly manages most of the sales and operations people for the services purchased by a particular customer group. That manager is now responsible for the profitability and return on equity of the division, which is also reflected in the manager's compensation.

With the objective of changing to a divisional, more customer-driven structure, bank officials had to consider how to change the structure of the organization with a minimum of disruption and a maximum of cooperation from a diverse group of employees, many of whom would feel alienated by some of the changes being made. These bank officials had a number of options in pursuing the restructuring, as Leonard Schlesinger and John Kotter pointed out in their article "Choosing Strategies For Change" (*Harvard Business Review*, March-April 1979). Schlesinger and Kotter argued that change is most likely to be resisted if people think they or the company will lose something of value in the process. If they perceive the price of change to be higher than the value they will receive from the change, if they do not trust management to look out for their interests, or if their general ability to adapt to changes is limited, bringing about change will be increasingly difficult.

In HBS's Organizational Behavior case analyses, students are constantly forced to be aware that there are two elements essential to formulating any plan for achieving an organizational change. First, one must have a clear objective. Second, one must understand the dynamics of the current environment—what is causing the existing problem, what resources one has available to bring about change, and what obstacles may stand in the way.

From this analysis, it becomes clearer what strategy is most likely to be successful. Then, consistent with the strategy, one must decide which actions to take given all of the elements one can control directly—*action levers*, in HBS parlance—on either an interpersonal or structural level to get the desired changes made. It is particularly important to choose a strategy and take actions that allow people to understand as quickly as possible what is in it for them.

Kotter and Schlesinger outline several strategies managers have available when plotting an action plan for change.

1. *Employee education:* educating others about the problem and the solution before the change occurs
2. *Participation and involvement:* soliciting the involvement of those needed to make the plan work and asking them to help you make the decisions about what actions to take
3. *Facilitation:* reducing people's anxiety about change by listening and giving emotional support, allowing time off, providing retraining plans and other possible assistance
4. *Negotiation:* giving something to a resistant party as an incentive to cooperate with the change
5. *Manipulation:* gaining cooperation by consciously structuring events so others have no choice but to cooperate
6. *Coercion:* getting people to do as one wants by threatening them either explicitly or implicitly with the loss of a job, a pay reduction, a non-promotion, or other subtle or not-so-subtle threats.

Two primary factors that shape a manager's perceptions of the organizational situation and of the most appropriate strategy for change are the culture and the business contexts. Culture is the much-talked-about intangible glue of an organization, the norms and values that people share about such things as how business should be done, how people should be treated, what behavior should be rewarded, and how conflicts should be resolved. Business context includes elements such as the industry, the competitors, economic conditions, the state of technology in the industry, resources available to the company and its competitors, the corporate goals of the company and its competitors, and key changes facing the industry.

HBS students are required to investigate five key questions prior to recommending a plan for acting to bring about organizational change.

Who?

Who are the stakeholders involved in the conflict or problem? What motivates them? What are their incentives? What are their perceptions of the problems and the possible solutions? Who will be hurt by allowing the situations to continue and who will be helped? To the people caught up in a problem, how important is it to solve it? How important to the manager are the people involved who must make the decision? How powerful are those people, and how can they affect the decision-maker in the future?

What?

What are the major issues of the conflict? Is the problem worth solving? What are the possible losses if the problem is not solved, and what are the gains if it is successfully solved? How importanat is it to solve this problem in relation to solving other problems and in terms of the effect the problem has on the day-to-day operations of the manager's territory?

When?

When does the problem need to be solved? Today? Tomorrow? Can it wait until next week? Will the problem cease to exist in a few days when a certain task has been completed? Will the problem set long-term precedents that could be damaging to any of the stakeholders, or to the manager not solving it?

Why?

Why has the desired outcome not already occurred? What are the factors that are inhibiting favorable results? Are there elements missing from the environment that should be added? Are there existing elements in the environment that are inappropriate?

How?

How likely is success? Is the investment of time and money likely to be worthwhile?

After answering these questions, many managers in the banking industry determined that the issues involved were worth all the time they could put into them, and were so far-reaching that the only way to even have a chance for success was to employ a strategy of educating senior management and employees about the urgent problems besetting the banking industry. That realization set the stage for soliciting everyone's participation in the planning for how to implement the necessary changes.

Some banks hired outside consultants to act as their agents for change. The consultants could ask the tough questions of the senior managers because they were not embroiled in the day-to-day relationships that were so critical to the continuation of business while change was being contemplated. The consultants gained their power to facilitate change from the legitimate power of the chairman's office and from their own expertise in the field.

At many banks, senior managers often spent up to two years in meetings with the consultants and with internal committees hashing out what businesses the banks wanted to be in, how to structure themselves accordingly, and how to implement needed changes in the organization as quickly and efficiently as possible.

By the end of two years, managers at all levels were very familiar with their redefined businesses, with the key success factors, as well as with what it would take in the future to maximize profitability in all areas.

Each person was then ready and motivated to implement the required changes in structure, operating systems, and management styles, and also to encourage the sharing of ideas and risk.

Bank chairmen whose strategy was one of educating and encouraging participation found that course of action helped to produce the best decisions and to implement those decisions smoothly. The people having input knew the competitors and customer marketplace, the culture and operational capabilities of the bank. Once the decisions were made, the managers who actually had to implement them were a part of the changes and were motivated to do what was needed.

But as senior- and middle-level management began putting agreed-upon changes into effect, many managers found that the toughest part of the job had just begun. Many banks found that getting old-line managers and nonmanagerial employees to change their attitudes and behavior was not easy. Lip service came easily, but real change did not. Close communication and carefully modified work and incentive systems grew increasingly important as tools to get desired changes understood, believed in, and implemented.

In many banks, one of the largest obstructions to change was the culture. Many bankers had come to believe that their jobs were for life and that their hours were strictly nine to five. Layoffs were a new and unwelcome phenomenon.

Lending officers, who had been encouraged for years to focus on enlarging their loan portfolio, now were asked to shift gears and try to load each customer relationship with as many of the bank's products as possible.

Employees were used to being paid based on seniority and hours, or on straight salary. Now many were compensated on production and contribution to the profitability of the bank.

Much of the work that managers were asked to do in the second phase of reorganization was to get employees in their divisions to understand the changes that were being asked of them, to commit themselves to these changes, and to work as members of a team.

ACTION LEVERS

HBS students are taught to consider carefully the *action levers* managers have available to them to influence others' behavior.

Two kinds of levers exist. Operating system levers are guidelines that can be institutionalized, like dress codes or bonus plans, to guide behavior. Interpersonal levers are methods of interaction that a manager can select from to deal with a particular situation. A description of action levers follows.

OPERATING SYSTEM LEVERS

Job Design. A manager must decide how production should be organized: Like a General Motors assembly line, where each employee has a narrow and specific task? Like a Volvo production team, each of whose members help build, and do quality control checks on, an entire car?

Performance Evaluation System. A manager must decide how often performance appraisals will be done, on what criteria an individual will be measured, and who will do the evaluation. Altered evaluation systems have been one effective lever in the banking industry to encourage employee behavior to change in the desired manner.

Incentive/Reward System. A manager must decide which performance will be rewarded and what form the reward will take. Both monetary and nonmonetary rewards can be powerful incentives to employee performance.

Recruiting Requirements and System. A manager must decide which types of people to recruit, which attributes to test during recruiting, who will do the recruiting, and how the right pool of potential candidates will be reached. Many banks have modified their recruiting guidelines somewhat in an effort to hire for their emerging needs.

Control System. A manager must decide which performance indicators as well as which plan variances are to be tracked.

Measurement System. There must be a system that tracks the kind of information needed to evaluate, reward, control, and plan.

Planning System. A manager must decide what information is needed to plan for the future, how this information will be gathered, how it will be digested and assimilated, who will do the work, and who will be responsible for meeting the goals of the plan.

INTERPERSONAL LEVERS

Management Style. Management "style" relates to self-management, including how one gathers information, runs meetings, relates to associates and employees, and even how one dresses. Style includes what medium of communication a manager uses most effectively and what kind of schedule he or she keeps. Different styles are effective in different situations and environments.

Communications Style. Effective communication means getting the point across so that people change their behavior. There are many ways to communicate, as we have already discussed, and will touch on further in the Management Communications chapter.

When thinking about how to communicate, consider the content of what you communicate, the medium, the tone, the timing and the sequence of communication, as well as the nature of the audience, and even your body language.

Communication style can have a major impact on getting cooperation from others and thereby getting what you want. Managers rely on other people to get things done; and being able to clearly and consistently communicate ideas in an appropriate manner is a critical skill.

Conflict Resolution Style. There are several options for resolving conflicts, including:

- bargaining, negotiating
- controlling the situation by—
  preventing or reducing the amount of interaction between conflicting parties
  structuring the interaction and not allowing certain kinds of questions and comments
  changing situational factors or pressures adding to or creating conflict
  counseling conflicting individuals personally
- confronting constructively and gaining an understanding of the issues at the heart of the conflict.

THE ACTION PLAN

A final management tool taught in the HBS OB course is that of the action plan. Students are asked to prepare a recommended action plan for each class based on the manager's position in the assigned case. A strong action plan must include—

- a summary of the problem
- management's key objectives
- management's recommended strategy
- recommended action steps, including—
  date and time of actions

specific actions involved
location of action
people involved
key points to be communicated
tone of interactions
the desired outcome
the expected outcome
anticipated problems
contingency plans.

While many experienced managers may argue that developing a detailed action plan is impractical or unnecessary, it forces HBS students to think carefully through the difficult case situations and take a stand on how they would attack the problem.

Class discussions often zero in on the relative merits of totally different approaches to solving the same problems. Almost always, many potential solutions exist. The best managers must learn to sort through the alternatives quickly to select action plans with a high probability of success given the situation at hand.

HBS cases dramatize that each individual is responsible in part for the human interaction within the company. Every person's behavior affects others, and the manager is hardly an exception to that rule.

Many people argue that managers are manipulators of other people. Beyond that, they argue, office politics is a counterproductive game. On the other side, there are those who argue that everybody comes out ahead if, as each person works in accord with self-interest, the corporation is also gaining. Manipulation is only as effective as the manipulator is at defining the "manipulatee's" self-interest. If the latter perceives that he or she is gaining from the situation, then there is no harm done. We are sure that this will be a never-ending controversy of general management.

We perceive it as positive that a school like HBS emphasizes the importance of OB. Many business schools are increasing their emphasis on the subject. Everyone is much better off if the managers of a corporation are sensitive to individuals' needs.

Employees gain through greater job satisfaction, feelings of self-esteem, and a sense of having ownership in the organization. The benefits to the corporation are lower costs, higher productivity, improved quality, and increased innovation. However intangible OB issues seem, their economic impact in the business world is without question.

ORGANIZATIONAL BEHAVIOR CHECKLIST

To quickly assess the effectiveness of Organizational Behavior policy and the likelihood for its success in meeting corporate goals, ask the following questions:

1. What are the goals of the organization, and of particular units? Are the units' goals well integrated with those of the entire organization?
2. Does the organizational structure fit with the strategy of the company? Does it facilitate the kind of behavior needed to meet the corporation's major goals?
3. Do the structure and operating systems minimize conflict and duplication of effort, while maximizing constructive communication and productivity? In particular, are the economic and noneconomic incentives designed so that what is good for the individual is good for the company, and what is good for the company benefits the individual?
4. Do people's skills, interests, and motivations match those needed to manage the organization's key success factors?
5. Are the right people in the right jobs?
6. Are people's roles clearly defined?
7. Is the company attracting and selecting the people needed to accomplish the tasks the organization must accomplish to succeed today and in the future?
8. Does management's style fit with the needs of the organization?
9. Does the culture encourage behavior required for the organization's success?

3

MARKETING

Marketing is one of the most talked about, loved, hated, respected, and misunderstood courses in the first-year curriculum at Harvard Business School.

Many students come to HBS with the misconception that Marketing is more of a gut-feeling, seat-of-the-pants discipline than are, say, Control, Finance, and Production and Operations Management (POM). Actually, as HBS classroom experience proves, strong marketing requires thorough analysis as well as sound judgment. Many students are caught off guard by the amount of detailed work required to make informed marketing decisions. The first-year HBS marketing course entails reading thirty-five cases, often thirty-five to fifty pages long, with up to fifteen pages of numbers to be crunched. Marketing cases are infamous at HBS for their length and complexity, and marketing faculty for their insistence on thorough quantitative analysis.

In our Business Policy chapter, we look at how students

learn the need for setting consistent policies in all functional areas of the company. Policy decisions made in the marketing area often set the tone for the entire organization. Marketing decisions determine what products a company is going to sell, how they will be positioned, whom they will be sold to, how they will be priced and distributed, and how their existence and special features will be communicated to the market. If these marketing decisions are not well thought out and intelligently executed, all the strategic planning in the world will still fail to yield acceptable corporate performance.

Going back to our analogy of sailing the corporate ship, a company's marketing director might be compared to the crew member who controls the ship's sails. Imagine the frustration of being in a corporate ship with the winds of economic opportunity howling when the marketing manager gets the sails up late, or changes them at an inopportune time, or just fails to trim them properly, leaving the rest of the crew to watch helplessly as the competition pulls ahead.

The first-year Marketing course drives home to students that having the right products at the right price and the right programs to effectively and profitably sell those products is one of the cornerstones of any successful business. The course at HBS covers the broad areas of consumer products, consumer services, industrial and international marketing.

In the second-year curriculum, each student can choose from a great variety of specialized marketing courses available, the better to focus in on an area of personal interest.

The first-year course follows a three-part sequence: an introduction to marketing concepts and methods of economic analysis; a look at the individual elements of marketing policy, such as product pricing, market selection advertising, and promotion; then the development and implementation of entire marketing plans.

Arguments over solutions to marketing cases are fierce even by HBS standards. So many possible recommendations exist— and of course we all like to think of ourselves as born experts in marketing.

Right from the first session though, students find that marketing cases generally require lengthy and thorough analysis of—

- The overall market and its more important segments
- Important competitors
- Present and potential customers
- The company and its products
- Distribution channels
- Advertising and promotion strategies
- Pricing strategies
- The marketing financials, particularly break-even points on recommended actions.

Given the detail required, Quantitative Analysis Jocks often do well early in the year. But beautifully crunched numbers often prove worthless if a student doesn't own any insight into customer needs and motivations. Consequently, many Humanists find openings to contribute strongly and many Synthesizers do well over the long haul because they are able to distinguish the forest from the trees that often clutter the pure analysis. At times, it can be all too easy to get lost amid the marketing numbers.

Marketing cases are enormously frustrating but true to business life in that they never contain all the information one would like to have in order to make a decision. HBS marketing professors make it clear that every great marketer is one who makes decisions based on thorough analysis, sound judgment and good instincts about human behavior. Many QA Jocks ultimately suffer calculator meltdown and tremendous irritation because the "right" marketing answers can never be found solely in the numbers.

WHO IS THE DECISION-MAKER?

Among the case-study situations students are asked to put themselves in as marketing decision-makers are—

- Vice-president of marketing for a small regional passenger airline confronted with a much larger competitor suddenly slashing its fares on the most important routes
- Director of marketing administration for an overnight package delivery service attempting to meet a corporate goal of increasing sales on a new product by 350 percent in 18 months despite sluggish introductory sales
- Vice-president of sales for an industrial pump manufacturer needing a pricing strategy for a relatively inexpensive piece of equipment (a strong competitor is expected to introduce a similar product within four to twelve months) that could save large companies hundreds of times its cost over a five-year period
- Communications manager for a major politician running for governor in a tough race, trying to decide how best to spend campaign funds to build awareness of and support for the candidate.

THE DECISION BEING MADE

By the yardstick named prestige, the marketing discipline seems to lose out in today's trendy, let's-get-results-now society to such other business areas as Finance, where results occur more quickly and can be tallied up less ambiguously in dollars and cents. But HBS sees marketing as one of the most important aspects of general management. Good long-term corporate direction is of little value to a company whose present products and marketing programs aren't capable of generating revenue and profits, and whose would-be consumers view the company's products as less attractive than a competitor's.

HBS places emphasis on doing a detailed analysis before making any recommendations. Marketing requires constant decision-making despite the inevitable uncertainties. Once made, many decisions are difficult to reverse. The marketing decision-maker must radiate confidence to move projects ahead. The more comprehensive the analysis done, the more confidently the analyst can make recommendations. Marketing analysis is an essential partner of judgment and instinct, not a stand-in for them, in developing recommendations that are intelligent and feasible.

THE MARKETING ANALYSIS AT HBS

Incisive marketing analysis, which can later be clearly and persuasively presented, goes far in shaping a marketing plan and directing the efforts of those who implement it.

There are at least three main supports to sound marketing recommendations: (1) understanding the nature of the market, (2) understanding competitors, and (3) understanding one's own company. These three factors must be seen accurately in detail before one can study more detailed components of the marketing system and develop recommendations.

ANALYZING THE MARKET

Understanding the marketplace that products are competing in is the critical first step. Among the important questions to be answered are, How large is the overall market? What is the growth rate of the market? How is the market currently segmented? Do trends point to any major shifts in market segments in the near future? Which segments are the company's products competing in currently, and what is the share of the market? What share of the market do the leading competitors have?

An important question HBS students are trained to ask while examining the market is, What are the key success factors in this business? Asking that question is a helpful way to focus on two or three areas of inquiry that should be considered in the marketing analysis and recommendations. Which factors have the most to do with determining the winners and losers in this business battle: product quality, product line diversity, pricing, packaging, distribution muscle, advertising muscle, constant introduction of new products, knowledgeable salespeople?

As an example, consider the cola wars. The two key success factors (KSFs) might well be distribution strength and adver-

tising clout. If called on to analyze a situation and make recommendations in this industry, one could waste time figuring
out who drinks cola, how to save money on ingredients, and
a whole host of other irrelevant factors. Such information is
meaningless to a company without a strategy to get the product
onto the overcrowded supermarket shelf and make consumers
instantly aware that it's there and worth trying.

In another industry the KSFs might be totally different. Who
will win and who will die in the auto industry during the
coming decade? Honda's sales steadily rose through the early
1980s, while Renault's declined—but not because of distribution strength and advertising clout. Development of a high-
quality product with the right features and the ability to manufacture it at the right price seem to be the KSFs auto industry
managers need to concentrate on today.

Finally, no market analysis is complete if one hasn't explicitly identified the most likely sources of future growth. Are
there new markets or new market segments to be entered? Is
the company's current market growing or can it be expanded?
Are new customers entering the market? Can the company
steal shares from competitors and if so from which ones? Can
current customers be encouraged to buy more?

The more accurately the current marketplace is understood
and potential sources of growth are identified, the easier will
be the job of developing successful recommendations.

ANALYSIS OF COMPETITORS

Developing a more detailed understanding of the competitors
one faces in the market is the second support beam of the
marketing analysis triumvirate. The questions one must ask
include, Who are the company's competitors? (The answer
requires differentiating between the strongest, most direct com-
petitor(s) and all others.) What are their objectives, resources,
and power? Which segments of the market are they targeting
today and where are they expected to be competing in the
future? How do they compare in terms of product quality,

price, distribution, and advertising and promotional expenditures?

The thorough analysis of competitors is stressed at HBS. An important goal is not only to understand a company's competitive environment today, but to know competitors' strategies, resources, and personalities well enough to predict future developments. The best marketers anticipate competitors' new products, future marketing programs, and likely responses to moves they are themselves considering.

ANALYZING ONE'S COMPANY

In the final and perhaps most important phase of the HBS Marketing course students are taught to analyze a company and its products in the context of the marketplace, assessing competitors to see where the company currently stands and what options are open to it in the future.

Key questions to do this analysis include, Where does the company stand in the marketplace in terms of size, market share, financial resources, historical performance, and current market position? Is the company dominant or a marginal participant? What are management's objectives and strategies? What resources can management employ to attain these objectives? What are the company's strengths and weaknesses compared to competitors and the industry's KSFs?

Areas that must be examined include product quality, product features, product value, pricing, distribution, sales-force strength, trade relations, advertising, and promotion. The best strategy recommendations must build on strengths and avoid reliance on areas where there is weakness.

Don't consider this analysis complete until it has been determined where the company is making its profits. That's not always easy to do. The banking industry, for example, is being forced by deregulation to identify the relative profitability of its many products and services so that it can charge fees where needed and channel growth plans into the most profitable areas. McDonald's, on the other hand, knows exactly where every penny it makes comes from. They practically chain customers' cars to the drive-through window until people buy french fries or apple pie because an intelligent marketer decided it cost nothing to ask for that order, yet the extra sales it generates are enormously profitable.

DEVELOPING PRELIMINARY RECOMMENDATIONS

With the three-part analysis complete, one can begin to develop the framework of a strong marketing recommendation.

The current situation is A. Key factors in the marketplace are B, C, and D. The range of options available to grow profitably include T, U, V, W, X, Y, and Z.

But to go further and pinpoint the best marketing plan possible from among all of the current options requires careful thought, judgment, and deeper digging into a number of critical areas that vary from situation to situation.

NARROWING THE OPTIONS

As HBS intends, confronting the cases forces students to pick out from the overwhelming, yet maddeningly insufficient, mass of facts and figures available those critical issues that must be explored more deeply to avoid unforeseen roadblocks and to test the merits of the available paths.

Areas that frequently need more detailed probing include brand position in the marketplace; consumer motivation and buying patterns; the distribution chain and which factors really determine which products are made available to the consumer for purchase (push strategies); the power of advertising and promotion to unleash buying power (pull strategies); the pricing options available that can affect both distributor and consumer response to the product; and finally the marketing math issues, which enable one to understand where a company makes its money, and to understand the financial implications of each possible marketing move.

POSITIONING ANALYSIS

How a product is positioned refers to how it fits into the mar-ketplace of competitive brands based on relevant criteria for comparison, such as product features, quality, price, image, and established reputation. If a brand does not differentiate itself in some way that is meaningful to consumers, it has little chance of success.

Distilling the position analysis to its basic elements, as the model below illustrates, there really are only two possible ways for products to compete: on the basis of cost, or perceived product differentiation by consumers.

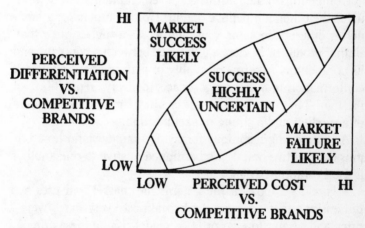

FIGURE 3–1. Cost Versus Perceived Differentiation Model

Competing on the basis of cost is one clear option. Having an equal or better product with a lower cost to retailers and to consumers can put a company in a powerful competitive position in many markets.

However, the effectiveness of a low-cost strategy depends on the importance of cost to the consumer in the market. The VW Beetle successfully competed on a cost-to-the-customer basis for many years. But many excellent IBM-compatible computers priced well below IBM's machines have failed miserably because customers were willing to pay a higher price (usually corporate money) for the security of a model made, and often serviced by, IBM.

Also, low cost can be delivered to consumers in two very different ways. Lower out-of-pocket cost is one way. A Ford Escort is priced lower than a Honda Accord; Ford trumpets that fact in its advertising. But in the eyes of many consumers the Honda actually has a lower total expected life cost because it requires fewer repairs and holds its resale value better than the Ford.

Competing on the basis of perceived differentiation of product is the other competitive option. Do consumers see a product as different in some ways and worth a higher price than similar products? Is there a difference between a company and its competitors in terms of quality of performance, quality of conformance (consistency), service, delivery, reputation, or prestige? These are all tools for creating strong differentiation of a product and a strong market position.

An interesting technique for trying to understand how various competitive brands are positioned relative to one another is the Positioning Map.

Figure 3–2 looks at the automobile market and uses two dimensions that are important to almost every car buyer— price and origin (foreign or U.S. made). Using these criteria, consumers clearly perceive products to be different.

Positioning maps can be drawn for any market and can be constructed based either on judgment or on market research. In either case, they are helpful in picturing where products currently are positioned and in identifying opportunities that exist to change the position of a current brand or to introduce a new product into a position niche currently open in the market.

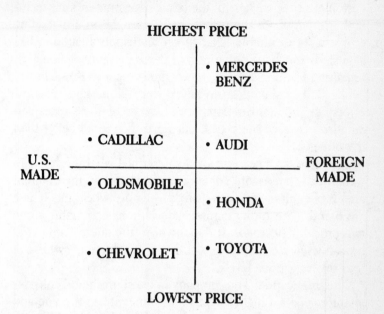

FIGURE 3-2. Hypothetical Auto Industry Positioning Map

CUSTOMER ANALYSIS

Analyzing the market is one way of thinking about who customers are and what their needs are. But defining and analyzing customers and potential customers can be taken far beyond just seeing the current market. A marketing analysis must determine what a product means to customers and it must identify the product needs of various segments of the customer population. Customers can be grouped using a number of variables, such as sensitivity to price, receptivity to advertising and promotion, preferences for types of stores, interest in buying well-known brand names, and demographic or psychographic characteristics.

HBS students are challenged to put themselves into the

customer's shoes. Many of the best class comments are seemingly simple observations that shed new light on a marketing problem. For example, after much discussion about an HBS case study involving a marketer of stereo equipment, the class remained confused about whether the company's limited marketing dollars should go to advertising, promotion, lowered prices, or product development. Dozens of break-even calculations covered the board, but no path seemed better than the others.

Suddenly, an Eccentric vividly described what it felt like to walk into a stereo store not knowing much about the different brands of equipment. She was right—it's overwhelming. There are brands with funny names, with buttons and features one will probably never touch. On a whim, the salesperson could probably sell a customer any of five or ten different systems at four different price levels.

The implication: The company in question should consider giving retailers a higher than average margin on the line and developing a program for building a strong relationship with sales personnel. Its limited marketing dollars might go furthest by encouraging salespeople to educate the customer about the company's product.

DISTRIBUTION ANALYSIS

Understanding the dynamics of distribution channels is critical. Toward that end, the marketer must answer a number of questions.

Does the product reach each segment of customers through a direct sales force, jobbers, manufacturers' representatives, distributors, or retailers? What is the profit margin and importance of this product for every individual in the distribution channel? How much incentive does each individual have to push our product? How does our distribution system compare with our competitors' systems? How can we make the present distribution system work harder for our product? Should we fundamentally change that system?

ADVERTISING/PROMOTION STRATEGY ANALYSIS

Advertising and promotion strategies play a major role in the marketing of many consumer and industrial products. Most companies hire an outside advertising agency and often a promotion agency as well to make sure that their advertising and promotion programs are carefully designed and executed.

Identifying the target audience—knowing who the current and potential customers are—is an important first step toward fine-tuning advertising and promotional programs. One wants to know how old the customers are, where they live, their income and educational levels, marital status, and the general characteristics of the neighborhood, city, and region they live in.

HBS students are also challenged to understand the target audience psychographically. What kind of an image do these customers have of themselves and what do they look for in the products they spend their money on? Are they ultra-serious or a little wild and crazy? Do they prefer well-established brands or do they want to be the first in their group to try things? Are they proud of wearing LaCoste shirts or would they feel less conspicuous walking naked in midtown Manhattan?

Once the target audience is clearly defined, the challenge is to select the right advertising and promotional vehicles to reach that audience. Television—expensive television—is wonderful for reaching large numbers of people with the impact of sight and sound. Radio reaches fewer people, but is less expensive and can be more precisely targeted because certain types of people listen to certain types of stations. Magazines can be even more highly targeted than radio for advertising. The man or woman who reads *Bon Appétit* is definitely interested in food; those who subscribe to *Car and Driver* probably are more into camshafts than caviar. Newspapers provide great immediacy and have fiercely loyal readers. For the company pursuing price-sensitive buyers, coupons, delivered through daily newspapers, separate mailings, or drop-off flyers, make a lot of sense.

It's enormously important to position a product in the marketplace so that consumers perceive it as we would like them to in relation to competitors' products.

In the world of imported automobiles Mercedes is positioned as very expensive, but very elegant and reliable. Porsche, also very expensive, is aimed more at the performance-oriented buyer. The Honda Accord is positioned as though it were a Mercedes for the middle class: moderately priced but luxurious, well engineered and with above-average reliability. The Mazda RX7 is positioned more like a middle-class Porsche, with a strong emphasis on styling, handling, and performance. The advertising campaign for each of these automobiles does an excellent job of communicating a well-chosen market position. And you can safely bet that in that process of self-selecting a niche in the marketplace, each company paid heed to strong market research.

For example, we said that Honda wants to be positioned as the Mercedes of the middle class. There were thousands of ways Honda could have tried to say that to people. Yet for many years they have summed up each of their television, radio, and print media ads with the same tag line: "Honda... We make it simple."

Many may argue that a stronger, more direct slogan, something catchy like, "Honda... the Mercedes of the middle class," would be better. But Honda's steadily increasing U.S. sales attest to the firm's correct assumption that their potential customers would understand the line to mean technologically sophisticated automobiles, devoid of gimmicks, built for comfort and durability.

If a company markets more than one brand, it must make sure all the advertising meshes without overlapping. It should not put its own brands in competition with each other. That can be difficult for general managers responsible for more than one brand or product line, and especially so for the manager with overall responsibility for an entire business. In an ideal world, every advertising and promotion dollar a company spends should in some way build upon all others spent by the corporation.

But that's an issue on which many highly successful companies differ. Procter & Gamble has thrived by keeping its many brands totally distinct from one another. Over the past several years, Nabisco has run separate television advertising campaigns for each of its brands but has tied them all together via a brief corporate signature announcement near the end of each commercial. General Electric, with its "We bring good things to life" campaign, has totally integrated its consumer product advertising in a highly synergistic manner.

Whether a company is spending too much, too little, or the right amount on advertising and promotion is an issue that almost always arises in HBS marketing case analyses. Unfortunately, no one at HBS or anywhere else has developed a formula to answer that question. The correct spending level in any particular situation depends on careful analysis of countless variables, including what a company's margins allow it to spend, how much competitors are spending, how difficult the message is to communicate, to what extent the advertising is "breaking through," and whether advertising is a key success factor for the particular business or product.

In most cases, HBS students do a break-even analysis on logical increases or decreases in ad spending to determine what options seem feasible.

PRICING ANALYSIS

Careful analysis of pricing strategy options on a regular basis is critical to forming optimum marketing programs. The price is one feature of a product that every consumer is aware of in deciding whether to buy or not.

Before asking specific questions to try to determine the product's optimum price, HBS students are forced to consider the range of possible prices. The lowest pricing option is the lowest cost the company can make the item at. If the price must be below that to be competitive, then the product should be taken off the market. At the upper end of the scale of possible prices is the item's *perceived value* to the target consumers. Pricing above this point would produce few sales.

Take the sale of a glass of champagne at Nippers, a champagne-only bar that is one of the hottest nightspots in Los Angeles and whose owners are in the process of expanding into other major American cities. Those people are faced with an interesting problem. Assume their bubbly costs them somewhere in the neighborhood of one dollar per glass. They can't price it at less than that and make money. But they seem to have created an environment where stars, aspiring stars, and want-to-be-near-stars are willing to pay almost any price to sip a glass at Nippers.

What should they charge? Price too low, and they're practically throwing money out the door. Price too high, and they may gradually diminish the appeal of the place and kill the goose that is laying the golden egg.

In one HBS case students were put in the shoes of the manager of a company that manufactures a piece of equipment for oil-drilling companies. The pump was new to the market and had no competition. Let's say it cost $1,000 to manufacture, but was so effective and durable that it had the potential to save well drillers in difficult climates $10,000 to $50,000 over a five-year period by minimizing equipment failures.

Also, the company is aware that a competitor is trying to have a similar product ready in six to twelve months. How should the pump be priced? Should it be priced low to try to gain volume quickly (a penetration strategy)? Should it be priced near the real value to the driller in order to make a killing even if the company only sells a few pumps (a skimming strategy)?

All hell can and does break loose in an HBS classroom trying to answer a pricing question like that. As in the real world, there is no clear correct answer, but there clearly is a logical analysis to be done. In addition to determining the low and high prices, students must find out how the current price compares with competitors' prices, and decide what the impact on sales would be if the company raised or lowered its price. How would a price increase or decrease affect profits, distribution levels, and distribution efforts? How would a price change affect the prices of competitors' products, and what impact would that, in turn, have on the first company's sales and profits?

With the answers to these questions in mind, the HBS student's job is then to recommend the pricing strategy that best fits with the cost structure and the long-term sales and profitability goals of the company—and then drop plenty of pencils in class until someone else is called on to open.

MARKETING FINANCIAL ANALYSIS

By now, it must be quite clear that HBS strongly emphasizes analyzing the numbers involved in any marketing decision in order to make economically sensible recommendations. And yet there is constant debate over when to bring marketing financial analysis into the picture. At HBS, many students find themselves often bogged down in the numbers. In making recommendations based on the detailed analysis we have outlined, it is necessary to check the validity of those recommendations based on the following marketing financial concepts:

Fixed Costs are those that remain stable whether a company's volume rises, falls, or stays the same. An independent insurance salesman pays the same rent for his office if he sells one, ten, or fifty policies.

Variable Costs can be traced to each incremental unit manufactured or sold. Every automobile that GM sells costs the corporation a certain amount for steel, tires, and glass, as well as for transportation to the dealer's lot.

Revenue is the total amount of money received for the sale of a good or a service.

Unit Contribution is the per-unit revenue or selling price minus the total variable cost per unit.

Break-even Volume is the volume at which the total contributions from all of the units sold equals the total fixed cost for the project.

The most common application of these concepts is the *break-even analysis*, which is used to test whether a possible marketing recommendation makes economic sense. The product manager on RC Cola must evaluate a recommendation from his advertising agency to increase ad spending by $10 million to keep up in the cola wars. He knows his unit contribution per case of RC is $1. He can easily calculate the break-even volume as 10 million cases. Is it realistic that the extra ads will generate that many extra cases in sales?

The strongest marketing recommendations consider realistic assumptions and risks so that, put into practice, those recommendations will very probably yield positive financial results. It is tempting to make aggressive, creative marketing recommendations without crunching the numbers to check their feasibility. In class, the risk is merely embarrassment. In the real world, the risk is unacceptable, however you calculate it.

THE COHERENT MARKETING STRATEGY RECOMMENDATION

After all of the analysis is done, the job of the HBS marketing student is not nearly complete. The last and most important task is to determine the implications of all of the analysis and make a concise, coherent marketing strategy recommendation. HBS students are always expected to make recommendations in class and to be prepared to defend them from attack.

Any marketing professional who has presented a recommendation to management knows what that position feels like. Based on the analysis only certain options are available. Based on the analysis and judgment only one direction is recommended. Having made a recommendation, there remains the task of communicating it and building agreement throughout the organization. The better the analysis, the more confident the recommendation. The more confident the recommendation, the more likely its acceptance.

In HBS classes and exams, the following basic components are expected to be included in every marketing strategy recommendation:

- A summary of critical points in the analysis that drive the recommendations being made
- An assessment of the company's strengths and weaknesses as they relate to the industry's KSFs
- A reasonable series of short- and long-term objectives for the company
- A recommended product strategy and a rationale, which discusses the product to be sold, its market position, and the targeted customer groups (It is critical that the recommendation be economically viable.)
- A recommended pricing strategy and rationale
- A recommended distribution strategy and rationale
- A recommended promotion strategy and rationale.

The components of an HBS recommendation must be internally consistent and must fit with the overall direction of the company. Recommendations must be supported by defensible analysis and judgment; all important assumptions should be identified. Each element and the program as a whole should be economically justifiable.

Last, but certainly not least, thirty-five year-one marketing cases at HBS teach students that recommendations had better make sense intuitively. If not, the recommendation stands solely on the basis of calculations, leaving the judgment of the presenter open to a blind-side attack. *If a recommendation doesn't feel right, think it through again.*

Marketing is still art as well as science and always will be. HBS stresses the science only to make sure it doesn't get left out. But the great power and joy of the discipline comes from creating the delicate mix of analysis and judgment.

MARKETING CHECKLIST

When evaluating a company's marketing strategies and programs, the following brief checklist of questions can be helpful in developing an HBS-style marketing analysis.

1. Does the company have a clearly defined strategy for successfully marketing its goods or services? A successful strategy must include—
   - clear short- and long-term goals
   - product policy
   - pricing policy
   - distribution policy
   - promotion policy.
2. Are these policies consistent with one another? Do they fit with the company's strengths and overall corporate strategy, and with the KSFs of the industry?
3. Does the current strategy anticipate short- and long-term competitive moves and other likely changes in the marketplace?
4. Do all the important players in the marketing arm of the company have clear direction and proper incentives to keep them working together?
5. Are the right people in place throughout the organization to successfully implement the recommended marketing objectives and strategies over the long term?

4

FINANCE

Having a good product and a solid strategy for getting it to market is only part of running a successful business. Another crucial part is having the appropriate resources to make the business more than just a good idea. To run a successful business there are three key resources that must be managed effectively: (1) financial assets, (2) production assets, and (3) human assets.

Harvard Business School's first-year Finance class is an introduction to business financial management, which involves determining how much money a company will need, how to get cash and credit, and how to use cash and credit to help meet the company's goals and objectives. The course gives students practice in using standard financial analysis techniques to answer three fundamental questions:

1. What investments and projects are attractive for the company to undertake?

2. How much money would be needed to fund these investments?
3. How should the money be raised?

Second-year elective courses go into much more depth in particular areas of finance. Those courses include Capital Markets—a study of the financial markets; Corporate Financial Management—a more in-depth study of corporate investment decisions and financing strategies; International Managerial Finance—a study of financial management within international companies; and Investment Banking.

At least 90 percent of every section of HBS students is completely in the dark for the first few weeks of the Finance course. The only ones who are relaxed are former CPAs and bankers who are familiar with the jargon and analytic techniques.

For us, the course started off with an assignment to do a monthly cash budget for a toy company with heavy Christmas sales. Students had to analyze the trade-offs involved in maintaining level production throughout the year or increasing production to meet the large seasonal demand. This was more than enough to terrify most people. At the professor's opening question, "Which production technique should the company undertake; how much money will it need and how should it finance that need?" much of the class slumped behind their name cards. It was going to be a long spring semester learning Finance by case study.

One famous HBS story came out of Finance. It was a few weeks into the second semester, when the Finance course is given, and, amazingly, no one in this particular section had yet passed when asked to open. It was like waiting for a no-hitter to be broken.

The class was meeting this morning to discuss a particularly complex case. The student called on to open was totally unprepared. Rather than panic, the man kept his cool. He removed his billfold from his pocket, flipped it open and said directly into it, "Beam me up, Scotty."

To this day, getting beamed up is not the thing to do, especially in Finance class.

Many non-HBS veterans wonder how a quantitative, technical subject like finance can be taught using cases rather than more standard teaching techniques like textbook readings, instructional lectures, and homework drills. Many HBS students, especially those with little prior training in finance, wonder the same thing.

"How can I do a case if I haven't been taught the techniques?" is a question asked frequently, and not merely rhetorically, early in the year. Most students, however, come to appreciate the strengths of the case-study approach. One may not come away from HBS Finance with the technical proficiency taught in standard finance courses, but one acquires a clear understanding through the cases of the important issues in managing a corporation's financial assets. As will become apparent in this chapter, students learn to assess alternative analytic techniques; to understand and manage financial assets; and to determine the impact of financial management on the corporation as a whole. Textbooks and instructional notes are available for students who need them, although those students must use the materials on their own time.

In Finance, HBS introduces students to the broad range of issues involved in financial decisions. Although it exposes students to finance theories and quantitative analytical techniques, HBS's objective is to graduate people who can identify the interrelationships between financial decisions and business objectives and strategies.

Although Finance is considered one of the "hard" courses in the HBS curriculum, it soon becomes evident that the "soft" quality of judgment is as important in this area of management as in any other.

It becomes clear that it is very important for financial managers to weigh strategic analysis and business policy concepts, the dynamics of the "five forces" in industry, and the company's strategic direction when developing financial strategies.

Business strategy and operating strategies drive both a company's need for cash and its ability to raise cash. Raising cash is much easier if the company is well positioned in its markets, has strong profitability, and has the confidence of creditors and investors.

Texas Instruments' strategy of being the low-cost producer in certain lines has been expensive to carry out, requiring major investments in capital, people, technology, research, and development. However, the success of that strategy has made it easier for TI to raise funds—cheaper funds than many of its smaller competitors. In effect, TI's strong business strategy and complementary financial strategy have worked to create a very strong competitive advantage.

This chapter reviews the decision-making processes and financial analysis techniques taught at HBS. Not surprisingly, the thought process for problem-solving in Finance is similar to that taught in other HBS courses, although the framework and specific analytic techniques are somewhat different. The process is one of analyzing the current situation, understanding its dynamics, knowing what the future cash needs will be given the company's objectives, then identifying the best course of action for raising the needed cash. Let's examine—

1. The role of the financial management decision-maker
2. The importance of financial management
3. The techniques used for analyzing financial decisions and the issues underlying those techniques
4. A checklist for assessing the appropriateness and effectiveness of any company's financial management policies.

ROLE OF THE FINANCE DECISION-MAKER

Throughout the course, students are placed in the shoes of a variety of financial decision-makers:

- A bank loan officer examining a prospective borrower. The loan officer must decide how much money that company would need to finance its sales growth, when it would need the cash, and whether the company is a satisfactory credit risk.
- The chief executive officer of a conglomerate with a strong appetite for acquisitions deciding how to reshape the company's capital structure now that it is strapped for cash and must meet large debt payments.
- The vice-president of finance of an innovative chemical company evaluating proposed capital projects and investments. The challenge is to decide how to finance those projects that will offer the best return on equity.
- The senior management team of a railroad company deciding how to exit a business: gradually shrink the business, sell the business as a leveraged buyout, sell it to the employees, or sell it to the public?

Many students are surprised to learn that there are many decision-makers and interested parties involved in the raising or investing of corporate funds. Concern about funds is not and should not be limited to financial managers and accountants. Managers in all functional areas of a business have a stake in the effective allocation of the company's financial resources.

THE ROLE OF THE CHIEF FINANCIAL OFFICER

Much of this chapter will be seen from the eyes of the chief financial officer (CFO), who is the the company's financial decision-maker or a major player in the decision-making process. The CFO's role is to maximize the value of the company by optimizing the company's cash flow. This requires establishing the cost and level of cash, timing decisions to meet cash flow needs, meeting internal and external restrictions, and identifying sources of funding. The CFO should establish strategy with objectives that facilitate achievement of the company's business objectives and its strategy.

One of the tasks involved in setting financial objectives is determining the *optimal capital structure* for the company. The *optimal capital structure* is the capital structure that maximizes the market value of the company. The optimal capital structure and the overall financial strategy depend on many factors, including the company's overall business strategy, the strength and power of its competitors, the nature of competition in the industry, and the values and risk preference of the management and owners. The CFO must constantly anticipate how much cash will be needed in the future so that today's decisions about how to raise cash do not impinge on the company's ability to raise more cash tomorrow at an acceptable cost.

The CFO, particularly in a large company, deals with many different people both within and outside the company. Insiders include the CEO; senior management; strategic planners; business unit heads; marketing, human resources, and production managers; and economic forecasters. Outside the company, the CFO deals with commercial bankers, investment bankers, portfolio managers, shareholders, and securities analysts. This job requires extreme sensitivity to the needs and interests of various constituencies. To perform well, the CFO must be a good communicator and a strong analytic thinker, with good foresight, who is well informed about factors inside and outside the company.

HBS stresses that all general managers in the company should be familiar enough with financial concepts to interpret the analysis upon which the CFO's and the financial managers' recommendations are based. All general managers should be able to question the CFO's analytical techniques and understand the strengths and weaknesses of each technique. HBS also makes clear that a CFO should be not merely a number cruncher, but an executive aware of a multitude of factors beyond the numbers, including—

1. The company's objectives and strategies
2. The competitors' objectives and strategies
3. The company's relative market position
4. The company's vulnerabilities and strengths
5. The company's current and future financial needs
6. Business, industry, and competitor trends
7. Competitors' financial position and capital structure
8. The macroeconomic trends
9. The capital market trends
10. The moods and concerns of the financial community and press.

The CFO's decisions regarding the amount of cash or credit a company will require, at what cost it can be obtained, when it is available, and when it must be repaid can have a major impact on the company's strength, flexibility, and cost structure. Corporate finance has an impact on how product prices are set, on how fast a company can change or improve its production process, on how much R&D it can afford, and on how much it can afford to pay its employees.

Even in a people-driven industry like advertising, a strong CFO is a necessity. One brilliant creative director or one exceptional new business development account manager can transform a talented agency from unknown to Agency of the Year in a short period of time. But to attract and keep those special people an agency needs the financial resources that only a talented CFO and sound financial management policies can produce. If the money isn't there to reward exceptional achievers, other agencies will buy them away.

When an employer hires a Harvard-trained MBA for a financial slot, even one many rungs below CFO, the company can take advantage of the scope of understanding that person brings to finance. The HBSer is able not only to crunch out five-year pro formas and weighted-average cost-of-capital calculations; but also to assess a company's financial assumptions, and ask questions and offer suggestions regarding strategies.

Some employers may feel this is overstepping the employee's bounds. Others will appreciate the input and encourage it. Employers should understand that the HBS-trained MBA has spent two years in classes designed to elicit strategic thinking through hard questioning and head-to-head confrontation. It is only natural for the erstwhile student to apply the same procedure in the work world.

THE IMPORTANCE OF FINANCIAL MANAGEMENT

Cash is one of the three major corporate resources, along with human and production resources. Like all other resources, if cash is squandered or hoarded, the company will perform below its capabilities or it will fail. But the real importance, it seems to us, is that good financial management can help a company reach its goals. Astute financial management can help a company compete more effectively in the marketplace and can even keep potential competitors at bay. It can also help create value for shareholders. The corporate financial management course offered at HBS in the second year goes into depth on how financial decisions can create value—decisions such as selling common stock when it is overvalued, repurchasing it when it is undervalued, and using that stock to finance acquisitions.

An excellent example of financial strategy creating shareholder value, at least temporarily, is that of LTV Corporation. In the late 1960s the management of LTV, a major conglomerate, raised its stock price from $6 to $100 per share by using creative financial management. From 1964 to 1968 the company purchased companies with low price/equity ratios using its maximum borrowing capacity. LTV then portioned out the acquisition debt to each of the newly acquired companies, sold a part of each company to the public and used the new equity to help pay down some of the debt. Then the company used the unused borrowing capacity of these new companies to finance other acquisitions. LTV's return on investment (ROI) and return on equity (ROE) were almost infinite because its real investment was so small.

Ultimately, the pyramid collapsed and LTV was forced to retrench significantly because it was unable to manage its chain of acquisitions effectively. But its explosive growth illustrates how strategic financial management can greatly enhance a corporation's business performance and shareholder value.

ANALYZING FINANCIAL DECISIONS

In the first-year Finance course, HBS students focus on three major areas of financial decision making:

1. *Investment Decisions.* Which projects should the company invest in? Projects might include buying a new piece of equipment, building a new plant, acquiring a company, or launching a new product.

   HBS students are encouraged to analyze proposed projects and investments from two points of view. The first is the strategic point of view. Does a proposed investment fit in with corporate objectives and with overall strategy? The second is the technical, or quantitative, point of view. Will the investment bring the company high enough return to justify the expense?

2. *Capital Management Decisions.* These decisions are called for in planning to carry out a company's business strategy. Two of the most frequently asked questions are, How much money is the company likely to need; and, When will the money be needed?

3. *Financing Decisions.* Which alternative financing plan should the firm use to raise the cash needed either for working capital or for investments? Should funds come from internally generated cash, equity, or debt, or from some combination of these?

LINKING FINANCIAL STRATEGY TO BUSINESS STRATEGY

Because financial strategy should be inextricably tied to business strategy, HBS students are taught to begin their analysis with a thorough understanding of the business and industry factors affecting a company. The objective is to understand what impact those factors may have on a company's financial strategy. This analysis also suggests what an appropriate financial leverage position and optimal capital structure may be. For example, the higher the business risk a company may have, the lower its financial leverage should be and the less debt there should be in its optimal capital structure.

Among the major questions that need to be addressed are the following:

- What are a company's objectives and strategies?
- What is the major business risk in this industry, and for a particular company in the industry?
- Which factors may cause need for cash in the future: growing sales, new product introductions, change in the production or distribution process, change in the profit margin, or delay in collecting receivables?
- What are management's objectives, strategies, and incentives?
- What is the ownership structure (public or private), and what are the owners' objectives and incentives?
- What is the company's financial position today and what is it most likely to be next year and over the next five years?

As HBS students dig into a case to analyze these questions, they are searching for the key financial issues that must be addressed. But they are also trying to define the context in which those decisions must be made. If the exact same amount of money is needed by two companies, the best recommendation for how to raise that money may be dramatically different for each, depending on the business context. A company in a highly volatile industry may best be served by issuing new equity, while one in a stable industry can issue debt and gain tax benefits, albeit with risk. A company whose most recent financial performance reports have been above analysts' expectations may want to satisfy all of its long-term cash needs immediately with a sale of stock; a company working its way through a period of heavy investment may benefit by borrowing only its minimum requirements today in hopes of finding a more favorable market for its equity down the road.

1. INVESTMENT DECISIONS

Deciding which projects to put the company's money in is an investment, or so-called *capital budgeting*, decision. When trying to decide whether or not to invest in a piece of equipment, another company, or in a product launch, analyze two key factors:

1. *Strategic Fit.* Does the investment make sense strategically given this company's present goals and strategy?
2. *Economic Return.* Will the investment provide an adequate return to make it worthwhile?

HBS teaches that a company should invest only in those projects that fit in with its business strategy and that offer a return on invested capital exceeding the cost of that capital.

STRATEGIC ANALYSIS

A cash-rich insurance company is contemplating buying a television station. The insurance company's strategy is to maintain the industry's best sales force, build business from word-of-mouth referrals, and become the lowest-cost producer in the business. It does little advertising. Although the television station may represent an interesting investment for some other company, it has no fit with, or synergistic value for, the insurance company. Compared to other possible investments, such as buying computers to automate underwriting and claims processing, or developing new products the sales force is clamoring for, the television station would be a poor investment.

ECONOMIC ANALYSIS

If the proposed investment clears the first hurdle, it faces the second, the technical analysis—and passes over that one, too, if the expected return on the capital invested exceeds the cost of that capital.

Essentially, the economic analysis is done by projecting the cash flow to be derived from the project over its life span and comparing the present value of those future cash benefits to the current cost of completing the project. The complicating factor is that all of the cash generated, even those dollars projected over many periods in the future, must be calculated in terms of the value of today's dollar, in order to account for the time value of money. The cash flow must be "discounted" according to the value of today's dollars. Calculating the correct discount generates debate, but at HBS the standard discount rate applied is the *weighted average cost of capital* (WACC).

Before discussing WACC calculation, let's digress for just a moment to explore the infamous and much talked about concept of *cost of capital*. This can only be a brief introduction to a subject that has been surrounded by controversy for years, and is still argued about for hundreds of hours each year in HBS classrooms.

CAPITAL AND THE OPTIMAL CAPITAL STRUCTURE

First, we need to define *capital* and the target or *optimal capital structure*.

Capital is the money that provides long-term financing for a company. Senior management must decide what percentage of debt they want in this capital base. The proportion of debt and equity they judge to be the most appropriate is referred to as the *optimal capital structure* (OCS).

The OCS is a guesstimate figure. In theory, the target amount of financial leverage should be based on a consideration of the amount of risk there is in the industry, the riskiness of a company's business strategy, the level of financial leverage that similar companies (called *twin companies*) are taking on, management's skill in meeting debt obligations as they come due, and the owners' preference for risk, or aversion to it.

As the amount of debt in a company increases, the company's cash value to the owners increases because of the tax deductibility of the debt interest payments. But, at the same time, the company's intrinsic value decreases because interest costs increase its risk of bankruptcy. A company that is heavily in debt cannot afford bad years because its debt holders have the right to foreclose. The optimal capital structure includes that amount of debt whose tax shield advantage just outweighs the increased risk of bankruptcy by just one dollar.

The most common means of setting a company's OCS is to examine carefully the capital structure of as many competitor companies as possible to see what percentage of debt and equity exists in each of their capital structures. Managers settle on a capital structure that seems normal or ideal for the companies they feel most comfortable emulating. Then they fine-tune their recommendation based on whether they feel that they can afford to take on the increased risks of higher debt or that they must be more cautious and maintain lower debt.

Companies in very stable industries, such as public utilities, tend to have far more debt than equity in their OCS. Equity is usually predominant in the OCS of companies that have a high risk of sales decline and bankruptcy, such as computer software firms.

Because the levels of debt and equity in any company's structure constantly vary, the OCS formulation is only a target. It is used as a benchmark to assist in planning how and when to raise cash, and also as a benchmark in conducting analysis.

DETERMINING THE WEIGHTED AVERAGE COST OF CAPITAL

Determining the *weighted average cost of capital* (WACC) is necessary before arriving at the OCS. The average cost of capital, in theory, is the average rate of return that capital investors expect the company to earn. Practically speaking, it is what it would cost, on average, to raise another dollar for the company. If a company used only bank debt to fund itself, the cost of capital would be the after-tax cost of borrowing another dollar. Since most companies have a more complex capital structure composed of both debt and equity, each of which has a different cost, the calculation of the average cost of the next dollar raised is very complex. The WACC is an attempt to approximate what the next dollar would cost if it were raised in the proportions of debt and equity targeted in the company's optimal capital structure.

The formula for calculating the WACC is shown in figure 4-1.

$$\begin{matrix}\text{WEIGHTED} \\ \text{AVERAGE} \\ \text{COST OF} \\ \text{CAPITAL}\end{matrix} = \left[\begin{matrix}\text{\% OF} \\ \text{LONG-TERM} \\ \text{DEBT} \\ \text{IN OCS}\end{matrix} \times \begin{matrix}\text{AFTER-TAX} \\ \text{COST OF} \\ \text{LONG-TERM} \\ \text{DEBT}\end{matrix}\right] + \left[\begin{matrix}\text{\% OF} \\ \text{EQUITY} \\ \text{IN OCS}\end{matrix} \times \begin{matrix}\text{AFTER-TAX} \\ \text{COST OF} \\ \text{EQUITY}\end{matrix}\right]$$

FIGURE 4–1. Weighted Average Cost of Capital Calculation

The cost of long-term debt, K(d), is the weighted average after-tax cost of the interest rate paid on debt.

K(d) = (weighted average of actual interest rate paid) times (1–corporate tax rate)

As an example, the K(d) for XYZ company that pays 10 percent interest on half of its long-term debt and 12 percent on the other half with a 48 percent effective tax rate would be calculated as follows:

$$[(10 \text{ percent} \times .5) \text{ plus } (12 \text{ percent} \times .5)] \text{ times}$$
$$(1 - .48) = 5.7 \text{ percent}$$

The cost of equity, K(e), is much more difficult to pin down. At HBS, the most talked about way to calculate K(e) is the *Capital Asset Pricing Model* (CAPM). We will not go into that in great depth. Instead, we will explain the fundamental theory, lay out the basic calculation, and let you argue the merits of the CAPM approach with your friends and associates.

In theory, the cost of equity should equal the rate of return stockholders expect a company to return on their equity investment (ROE). This expectation is based on their perception of how much risk their money is at while invested in a particular company. The CAPM captures this theory, elaborated below, in the following algebraic model.

$$K(e) = R(f) + B[R(m) - R(f)]$$

The variables in the model capture mathematically the various risks that an equity holder wants to get compensated for when investing in a company. R(f) represents the "risk-free" rate of return expected from securities such as treasury bills. With these, the default risk of the issuer, the U.S. government, is negligible. The expected return is related to the expected rate of inflation and the going interest rate during the time period of the investment.

[R(m) − R(f)] represents the market risk premium of the extra risk that an investor incurs by investing in the general stock market, such as the Standard & Poor's 500 stocks, instead of risk-free treasury bills. This premium has averaged 10 to 12 percent over the last thirty years.

Beta ("B") is a measure of risk based on the volatility of a company's stock compared to the general stock market. Beta is 1.0 if the company's risk is average, if its stock price moves almost exactly in parallel with the Standard & Poor's 500 index. If a company's stock price is less volatile than the general market, such as a utility stock, its beta will be less than 1.0. A company whose stock price is extremely volatile, such as a computer software firm or biotechnology company, may have a beta closer to 2.0.

Many hours of discussion at HBS revolve around how to calculate each of these variables; given that they change, it is difficult to measure investor expectations. Historical rates may not accurately reflect future expectations, and beta changes with the financial leverage of a company. Amid the confusion, it became clear to us that it is important to understand the rationale behind the CAPM theory and the effect of assigning one value to a variable. However, the controversy will continue.

If XYZ company's beta is 1.2, the treasury bill rate is 8 percent, and the return expected in the stock market is 12 percent, XYZ company's K(e) is 8 percent + 1.2(4 percent) = 12.8 percent.

If XYZ company's optimal capital structure is 50 percent debt and 50 percent equity; and if K(d) = 5.7 percent, and K(e) = 12.8 percent, then the WACC would be 9.25 percent calculated as follows:

$$(.50 \times 5.7 \text{ percent}) + (.50 \times 12.8 \text{ percent}) = 9.25 \text{ percent.}$$

USING THE COST OF CAPITAL TO MAKE AN INVESTMENT DECISION

Now, back to making investment decisions. The theory is that the expected cash flow from a project should be discounted back to its value in current dollars, which is calculated using the WACC formula. This is a *discounted cash flow analysis* (DCF).

Clearly, if the present value of the future cash flow does not exceed the present value of the cost of the project, the *net present value* (NPV) is negative and the project will not provide returns big enough to meet investors' expected returns. It will cost more to raise the funds than they are worth.

If, however, the present value of these cash flows does exceed the present value of the cost of the project, then the NPV is positive and the returns generated by the investment meet the investors' economic requirements.

To calculate a discounted cash flow, HBS students are taught to project what they estimate the net free cash flow to be over the life of the investment. Below is one possible approach to conducting a DCF.

XYZ company has $4,000 to invest and is trying to decide which of two investments it should choose. The CFO projects the anticipated net cash flows on each as follows:

Net Annual Cash Flows

Investment	Year 1	Year 2	Year 3	Year 4
A	−$4,000	+$2,000	+$2,000	0
B	−$4,000	+$ 500	−$ 500	+$6,000

Initially, the president of the company thought investment A would be best because the payback on it was only two years. However, when the CFO calculated the net present value (NPV) of each by discounting each cash-flow stream back at XYZ's WACC of 9.25 percent, it was found that investment B was the wiser investment. The CFO's calculations were as follows:

$$\text{NPV of A} = -\$4,000 + \frac{\$2,000}{(1.0925)(1)} + \frac{\$2,000}{(1.0925)(2)} + \frac{\$0}{(1.0925)(3)}$$
$$= -\$4,000 + \$1,831 + \$1,676 + \$0$$
$$= -\$493$$

$$\text{NPV of B} = -\$4,000 + \frac{\$500}{(1.0925)(1)} - \frac{\$500}{(1.0925)(2)} + \frac{\$6,000}{(1.0925)(3)}$$
$$= -\$4,000 + \$458 - \$419 + \$4,601$$
$$= +\$640$$

In this example, investment A actually has an NPV of −$493. Given its WACC of 9.25 percent, the investment costs XYZ company more than it will return. Based on the economic analysis, it's not a sound project for the company.

Investment B has a positive NPV of $640. XYZ could raise $4,000 of capital at a weighted average cost of 9.25 percent and get a positive return on the project. Based on the numbers, project B is worth recommending.

HBS students are continually asked to check their quantitative results intuitively. In this example, the numbers make sense.

Given inflation, few of us would hand someone $4,000 today only to get back $2,000 next year and $2,000 more the following year. That's what investment A offers the XYZ company. In the case of investment B we have to wait until three years out to get a big return, but $6,000 back on $4,000 could offer positive NPV.

If strategic analysis is done first so that only those projects that are strategically sound are evaluated quantitatively, and if all future results of the investments, such as production or distribution synergies, are being factored into the cash flow projections, then an appropriate way for the CFO and management to decide which investments or projects to spend available dollars on is to invest in those with the highest positive net present values.

In this way, WACC is used as a "hurdle rate" for capital budgeting; WACC is the rate that projects must return in order to meet investors' requirements. If projects return less than this rate, theory says, investors would be wise to invest somewhere else.

Some theorists believe that dividends should be paid only by companies that have available dollars but no available investment options that would return a positive NPV. A company that pays dividends but leaves undone projects with a positive NPV is doing a disservice to its investors and is reducing their wealth. By definition, investors would not have their money in the XYZ company with a WACC of 9.25 if they could be getting higher rates of return elsewhere.

The same project may be evaluated differently by different companies depending on how they calculate the cost of capital, develop assumptions about anticipated costs and benefits, and assess their demonstrated or (as they may see them inherent capability to reap benefits from a project.

VALUING AN ACQUISITION

Perhaps the project in Finance class that best captures the HBSer's imagination is the mock acquisition negotiation that brings these concepts to life. The potential acquirers try to determine the present value of the expected cash flow of the target company. The target company tries to make this same judgment about its worth to the acquiring company and won't accept less money than that. The target has great incentive to find a buyer who sees the most potential in it because it will be able to get the most money from that buyer. A number of potential buyer groups are formed in each section and the target group negotiates with whomever it chooses. If a point is reached where each side believes it's getting a deal of positive economic value, a merger is agreed upon. If agreement can't be reached, the players part company and look for other partners to satisfy their objectives.

2. CAPITAL MANAGEMENT DECISIONS

Once the company has gone through its list of potential investments and has decided which ones it would like to fund, the next questions to answer are, How much cash will be needed and when will it be needed to fund these investments as well as ongoing operations?

PRO FORMAS

To determine how much money a company needs, HBS students learn to do projections known as *pro formas*.

Cash-flow pro formas are an effective way to analyze the effect all of the desired investments and transactions may have on the company's appetite for cash. Pro formas can be done on a daily, weekly, monthly, yearly, or on a multi-year basis. The usual method of developing a cash-flow pro forma is to calculate the level of assets, expenses, and debt repayment that needs to be financed. Then the analyst looks to where the company can get the cash. HBS students learn to estimate first how much cash will be generated internally from operations; this is done by projecting a likely income statement scenario based on historical performance and expectations for the future. This calculation may look like the following:

PRO FORMA INCOME STATEMENT

	Year 1	Year 2	Year 3	Year 4	Year 5
sales – cost of goods sold					
gross profit – operating expenses					
earnings before interest and taxes – interest expenses					
profit before taxes – taxes					
profit after taxes – dividends paid out					
change in retained earnings					

This forecasted change in retained earnings is then plugged into a pro forma balance sheet, which is also based on historical performance and expectations for the future. A simple pro forma balance sheet may look like the following:

PRO FORMA BALANCE SHEET

Assets:	Year 1	Year 2
cash		
accounts receivable		
inventory		
net fixed assets		
other assets		
Total Assets		

Liabilities and Equity:	Year 1	Year 2
accounts payable		
accrued expenses		
long-term debt		
capital stock and additional paid-in capital		
retained earnings		
liabilities and equity subtotal		
Total Liabilities and Equity		
Other funding necessary		

One of the primary objectives in the first-year Finance course is learning how to calculate the "other funding necessary" line.

A brief summary of how to begin projecting each line of the pro forma balance sheet is outlined below.

Cash: Project cash based on minimum anticipated operating needs.

Accounts Receivable: Project receivables based on historical outstanding receivables as a percentage of dollar sales adjusted for any expected changes in the speed of collections.

Inventory: Project inventory based on historical levels as a percentage of unit sales adjusted for any expected changes in the level of inventory required.

Net Fixed Assets: Project these assets based on the level at the analysis date, plus capital expenditures projected, minus depreciation that will occur, minus the book value of any projected sales of fixed assets.

Other Assets: Project other assets based on the level at the analysis date plus any other assets the company anticipates acquiring, such as a patent secured or a loan made to an affiliate company.

Total Assets: This is the sum of all projected assets.

Accounts Payable: Project accounts payable based on historical levels as a percentage of inventory purchased, adjusted for any expected changes in the trade terms available.

Accrued Expenses: Project these expenses on historical levels as a percentage of sales or operating expenses, adjusted for any expected changes in trade terms available.

Long-term Debt: Project this debt based on the outstanding amount at the analysis date, minus amounts due to be repaid by the projection date, plus amounts under negotiation that will be taken down by the projection date.

Capital Stock and Additional Paid-in Capital: Project these amounts based on the level at the analysis date, plus the market value of stock already decided to be issued by the projection date minus the value paid for shares projected to be repurchased by the projection date.

Retained Earnings: Project retained earnings based on the level at the analysis date plus or minus the forecasted change in retained earnings indicated in the pro forma income statement.

Liabilities and Equity Subtotal: This is the sum of all projected liabilities and equity listed.

Total Liabilities and Equity: This equals the level of the total assets projected on a balance sheet.

Other Funding Necessary: This is "the answer." Other funding necessary equals the liabilities and equity subtotal, minus total liabilities and equity. This is the amount of money required to finance all of the company's projected activities. If this figure is negative, the company is projected to generate more cash than it has planned to invest. Then it's back to the investment-planning drawing board.

Under time pressure during an examination, HBSers reach the answer and move on to decide how to finance the projected cash needs. But they learn, often painfully, they should not move so fast. Although the answer looks like a hard number, it is built on the soft ground of assumptions that need to be tested through sensitivity analysis.

SENSITIVITY ANALYSIS

Pro formas are nothing more than guesstimates about what is likely to happen in the future. They are forecasts based on well-educated assumptions. HBS students are taught to ask themselves what happens if the assumptions change. Sensitivity analysis is the financial term for examining the pro formas in several "what if" scenarios to see which variables will have the strongest effect on the financial picture. HBS encourages students to use their judgment as to which variables the projections are most sensitive to, and then to test the impact of change by doing a best-case and worst-case scenario.

The worst-case picture—the situation in which the project is no longer economically viable—is the most interesting. If it's not all that unlikely to materialize, the company's plans should be reconsidered. The best projects are those that make sense even when the future turns out worse than forecast.

Financial analysts frequently use sensitivity analysis to help them understand how potential opportunities and risks may affect a company's financial performance. Pro forma analysis enables the CFO to assess the range of financing needs that may have to be met. The best financial managers are every bit as interested in the potential high and low amounts of cash they may have to finance as they are in the best-guess amount. Maintaining financial flexibility in order to meet all of the company's possible future financial needs is an important part of the CFO's responsibility.

3. FINANCING DECISIONS

After determining through the technical analysis how much cash is needed and when it is needed, the next step is to identify the best source for obtaining the funds.

A CFO can generate funds from within the corporation by managing assets, liabilities, and earnings appropriately.

On the asset management side, collection of accounts receivable can be hastened; inventory turnover sped up, productivity improved (to generate more sales on a constant asset base); equipment or other assets sold; or a portion of the business divested. Managing the liabilities to slow down the payments to suppliers or to lengthen the maturity of bank debt would also generate cash. Cash could also be raised by increasing prices or reducing expenses and thereby raising profits. And more profits could be retained for corporate use if dividend payments were reduced or deferred.

The availability of internally generated cash is somewhat dependent upon how tightly run the operations are on a day-to-day basis. In a well-run company, it may be difficult to manage the assets, liabilities, and earnings more closely. And, there are risks. The company may lose sales by asking its customers to pay more quickly. Creditors may begin to question the company's credit-worthiness if payments are slowed. What would the market think if dividends were cut? So, although it's possible to generate more funds than had been anticipated, it would likely be a move of last resort for many companies, especially for a company running with little slack.

The external sources of cash available to a CFO are primarily debt, equity, and hybrids of these two.

Debt could be raised on either a long-, medium-, or short-term basis. And it could be "senior," having a first claim on cash flow and assets as agreed by contract, or "subordinated," having secondary claim. Because debt is negotiated, the CFO can attempt to set the most advantageous contractual agreements and convenants that the creditors will agree to.

The most common forms of equity, and most discussed in first-year Finance, are preferred stock and common stock. And the most frequently discussed hybrids are convertible debt—debt with an accompanying right for the holder to convert it into common stock at a particular price in the future—and debt sweetened with warrants. The latter allow the holder to buy common stock in the company at a particular price at a given time in the future.

Before doing a thorough technical and qualitative analysis to determine which funding mechanism would make the most sense, HBS students try to limit the options to the few funding vehicles that *may* be sensible. A company with earnings power large enough to cover interest payments; with strong and predictable cash flow; with asset quality to repay the debt principal;

and with financial leverage below that targeted by the optimal capital structure would likely try to raise debt. This is usually the cheapest source of external financing. But the price incurred with debt is that it must be repaid within a particular time. And restrictive convenants about which actions the company can and cannot take may reduce management's and owners' control.

The CFO of a company that would rather issue equity is one that wants to reduce the financial leverage, perhaps because of being all borrowed up or because of potential business risks. Or, perhaps due to an investment in a very-long-term project, the CFO may want to bring in permanent capital that will never have to be repaid.

The time when it may make sense for a company to issue convertible debt or debt with warrants is when its stock price is extremely low given future expectations. By issuing and making the stock available at a higher, more reasonable price the company's ownership is not diluted by selling stock at the low price. If the company does well, the debt can be transformed into equity and the debt obligation disappears. If the company does not do as well as expected, however, the debt burden will remain and could become onerous.

Many HBS students use an analysis framework called FRICT to analyze the potential of each funding vehicle in a given situation and to set a strategy for making financing decisions over several years.

FRICT stands for—

FLEXIBILITY
RISK
INCOME
CONTROL
TIMING

Students analyze each funding vehicle and funding source in terms of those five factors and in relation to a company's objectives, strategies, current financial condition, optimal capital structure, and future cash needs. Within the FRICT framework, the following questions give a sense of the elements HBS students consider when deciding which funding vehicle makes sense.

FLEXIBILITY

How many financing options are really open now and how many should be kept open for the future? Is the bond market a viable alternative given a company's rating? Is the equity market available? Should equity be issued now so that in the following year a second round of financing could be done with debt, given the lower leverage position? Does one source make more sense than another, given transaction costs, the size of transactions, the time frame within which cash is needed, and the company's financial condition? In selecting one source over another, how is the company's financial flexibility affected compared to competitors'?

RISK

How much financial risk (debt) can the company afford? How much financial risk is desirable given business risk, business strategy, bond rating, quality of earnings and assets, leverage and liquidity position, and predictions for interest rates?

INCOME

What effect would each type of funding have on income, earnings per share, and cash flow after interest and dividends? What would the effect be on the price/earnings ratio and the stock price in relation to that of competitors? Could obligations be met as they come due?

CONTROL

In considering debt, would the required convenants be too restrictive? Would default be likely under existing covenants and force the loss of control to creditors?

In considering equity, to what extent would current ownership be diluted?

TIMING

Which of the vehicles would bring the actual capital structure more into line with the optimal capital structure? Given current economic and capital market conditions, is one source of funding more attractive than others? Do future expectations for interest rates make one vehicle more attractive than others? Are there any particular funding vehicles or sources in vogue, as junk bonds were in the first half of 1985? How much more would the banks charge to allow less restrictive covenants at this time? Will one source that is available today be less accessible in the future?

HBS FINANCE: THE BIG PICTURE

The first year of Finance at HBS covers an enormous amount of ground. If the few fundamental concepts covered in this chapter seem overwhelming, imagine how students feel as they try to crunch enough numbers and analyze enough issues to make a major financial decision night after night. But by the end of the course, many HBSers are amazed at themselves for having absorbed so much.

FINANCIAL CASE ANALYSIS

Students may be asked to put themselves in the shoes of the financial vice-president of a regional Texas steel company looking to expand over the next three years. The financial vice-president must make recommendations for a financing program by the end of the month.

An HBSer's situation analysis and action recommendations are expected to include the following:

- An executive summary of the recommended financing program and supporting arguments

- A summary of important issues about the business and about industry risks and opportunities that have an impact on the financing decision
- A recommendation and rationale for the optimal capital structure
- A projection of how much money is likely to be needed and when (The students first produce a pro-forma income statement and balance sheet for three to five years to calculate the financing needs; to make underlying assumptions clear; and then to conduct a sensitivity analysis that tests the possible cash savings if assumptions are too pessimistic and less cash is needed)
- A recommendation and rationale for how the expansion should be financed over the course of the three years (This part of the analysis includes a recommendation and rationale for the sequence of debt, equity, or hybrid financing vehicles that should be used).

Although the above points answer the question posed in the case, a real Finance Jock would seek extra points by doing valuation of the firm with a discounted cash flow analysis, assuming the expansion does occur as planned. That would help to clarify whether the investments required to expand would actually enhance the value of the firm.

CONCLUSION

Although such financial decisions require heavy quantitative analysis, there is no single correct course of action. The primary goal of HBS first-year Finance is to enable students to understand the issues involved in financial management, and to give students the capability to dig into problems by applying fundamental analytical techniques—and, through that process, to help students become familiar with possible solutions.

FINANCIAL MANAGEMENT CHECKLIST

In order to know whether one is maximizing the value of a company by making appropriate investment, capital management, and financing decisions, ask the following questions:

1. Are the company's financial objectives and strategies consistent with the overall business objectives and strategy of the company? In particular, do the financial strategies reinforce the company's main strategies for differentiating itself from and staying ahead of its key competitors?

2. Is the company's financial performance adequate to support the people and programs necessary for the company to obtain its short- and long-term goals?

3. Does the company have a system for analyzing investment proposals that takes into consideration both the strategic value and the economic value of the investment in relation to the cost of capital required to fund it?

4. Does the company have the appropriate amount of cash available for ongoing operations? Is it able to meet obligations in a timely manner?

5. Does the company's capital structure approximate an optimal capital structure given the business risks, and the objectives and risk preference of the management and the owners?

6. Do the decisions regarding the company's method of funding reflect an appropriate balance of flexibility, risk, income, control, and timing?

5

PRODUCTION AND OPERATIONS MANAGEMENT

To this point, we have dug into four of the major issues involved in operating a business.

First, in Business Policy, we decided what it is that the company wants to do. Second, in Organizational Behavior, we wrestled with how best to organize a company and manage its employees in order to accomplish business goals. Third, in Marketing, we determined what it is we want to sell and at which target group we want to direct that sales activity. Fourth, in Finance, we figured out to some degree how to pay for the earlier decisions.

Now, we must answer the really difficult question: How the hell are we going to make it?

That's the job of those who specialize in production and operations management.

As we have said, the Harvard Business School system stresses that all general managers must know how production and operations fits into the business as a whole, although the nitty-gritty day-to-day production decisions can often be left to specialists.

In many ways, production and operations management is the orphan of business management. Not many students arrive at HBS, or at other business schools for that matter, with a background in production and operations; and relatively few plan to enter the field after graduation. That can mean some wild class discussions at HBS, as students pretend to be experts in areas they know nothing about. Fortunately, in each HBS section there are likely to be three or four students with relevant work experience in the production and operations management decision-making process. Also, Production and Operations Management professors at Harvard are well known for being especially intolerant of unsupported classroom contributions and unsubstantiated recommendations in written work.

Most students at HBS know Production and Operations Management by its acronym, POM. All students know it as a lot of work, a course where detailed analysis involving crunching reams of numbers must be done before any kind of meaningful recommendations can be made.

The greatest marketing plan in the world coupled with strong financial management will be wasted if a company can't make the right product at the right time and the right price, or if it can't deliver it to the right place day after day and month after month. The production end of a business isn't glamorous, but it requires the ability to make what are often complex decisions.

In the small-car market in the 1980s, GM, Ford, and Chrysler may have good-looking designs, strong dealers, excellent marketing, and deep pockets. But if their small-car products roll off the assembly lines with a price tag $1,500 to $2,000 above their foreign competitors and with many more quality-control problems, there will probably be a Toyota, Nissan, or Honda in most Americans' garages by 1990. There may even by Hyundais or Yugos.

The HBS case-study method is well suited to teaching Production and Operations Management. POM cases tend to be long and packed with data about various companies' production facilities, employees, and processes. Cases also include information on some of the issues managers are confronting. Usually it is up to the student to assemble first a clear picture of the whole production process and then to analyze it from the information available in order to determine what problems seem to exist, the cause of the problems, and the possible solutions—and only then to go about choosing an alternative solution and making a recommendation.

The POM course looks at production and operations issues associated with both manufacturing and service industries. Over the course of a year, HBS students learn that many concepts applied to producing cold, hard steel by the ton for industrial customers also have application for serving fresh, hot hamburgers to hungry customers at a fast-food restaurant.

Specific tasks covered in the first-year POM course include the following:

- Diagramming and analyzing the production process
- Analyzing the structure, strengths, and weaknesses of various types of production methods
- Managing production capacity
- Scheduling and utilizing existing capacity
- Planning for the acquisition and introduction of new-process technology
- Improving existing production processes and current production quality
- Developing strategy for manufacturing/technology that is appropriate to the company's overall corporate strategy and integrating it into that strategy.

Efficient production and operations isn't all buildings and machines; POM cases at HBS integrate human, economic, and technological issues. Students are taught that modern managers must judiciously weigh these three types of issues in the process of developing strong production and operations policies that meet organizational goals for product quality, cost, and customer service; and that fulfill responsibilities to workers and to the outside community as well.

As HBS cases try to show, strong production and operations management is a crucial factor in a company's long-term success. Concepts get turned into tangible products via POM policies and programs. POM decisions directly affect the size, shape, quantity, quality, price, profitability, and speed of delivery of a company's output, whether the company is the producer of an industrial product such as steel, a consumer product such as automobiles, a new high-tech product such as computer-aided design equipment, or a service such as fast food. That is *not* Ronald McDonald back there cooking, we discovered.

The importance of sound POM becomes even more apparent when two other factors are considered.

First, most companies must live for long periods of time with their major POM choices. Production systems are very difficult to change once set up. The capital costs of installing new factories and new machinery, as well as the time involved in training an organization to run the new system once it is installed, dictate that future changes must be minimized, even if results are not 100 percent up to expectations.

Second, once a system is in place, it tends to dictate which new products or services the company can easily consider in the future. Every type of production system has its strengths and its limitations.

If a company sets itself up to produce an item in high volume at low costs, it will probably not easily be able to go into business areas that require more customized services. A company set up from the start to deliver small quantities of customized products will probably be unable to successfully compete for high-volume orders. For example, many American shoe manufacturers who set up their operations to manufacture high-quality, hand-sewn shoes in relatively low volumes are now finding it impossible to compete in the mid- to low-price segments of the market where high-volume foreign makers dominate.

Given these facts, it is obvious that effective management of production and operations is a critical success factor in most businesses. POM issues should be addressed carefully at the highest level of corporate decision-making; POM plans should be thoroughly integrated into the company's overall strategic blueprint, and attended to by the best and brightest managerial talent.

But the reality in American business over the past several decades has been almost the opposite. POM decisions have too often not been incorporated as priorities in corporate strategic planning. Instead, production and operations divisions have been asked simply to react to predetermined strategic plans. Positions in production have lagged behind those of marketing and finance in terms of salary and prestige in many companies and, not surprisingly, the disciple hasn't attracted the quality and depth of fresh managerial talent needed.

The result of the long-standing lack of care, attention and strategic focus in the POM area has been disastrous for many American businesses. The U.S. share of total world output plunged from 52.9 percent in 1960 to 36.29 percent in 1979. Over that same period Japan, whose attention to manufacturing detail has become renowned, increased its share of world output by 8.3 percent. The soaring U.S. trade deficit is another tangible sign of America's loss of manufacturing competitiveness in comparison to other industrial and developing nations. We need only think of the rising sales of imported automobiles or the closing of steel mills throughout the U.S. to see clearly the dramatic negative impact of outdated, ineffective POM.

Many elements have interacted to relegate production and operations to so low a priority in American business.

- During much of the 1940s, 1950s, and 1960s, many companies' major focus was on producing as much as possible in order to meet the demands of an expanding market. Companies have been slow to respond to the increasingly competitive world environment, which now requires more attention to the operating and manufacturing function in order to be successful.
- Operations managers are generally stereotyped by top man-

agers as technicians and engineers. Often they are wrongly judged as being uninterested in and incapable of involvement in the larger corporate issues, so they are not invited to participate. On the flip-side, managers outside the production area, often including top management, are not encouraged to interact with production personnel or to learn about the production process and its place in the corporate strategy. Instead, top management often elects to delegate responsibilities in these areas to the increasingly isolated specialists.

- Many business schools have compounded the problem by deemphasizing the whole area of operations and manufacturing, or by stressing only fancy technical theories, like linear programming and queueing techniques, rather than emphasizing the management and problem-solving techniques needed to master, coordinate, and motivate all of the individuals involved in the production process.

In the first-year Production and Operations Management course HBS attacks a number of these problems directly.

WHO IS THE POM DECISION-MAKER?

Each night, eighty-five students in each HBS section are put into the shoes of a hypothetical production manager and asked to deal with that manager's specific operations problems. Those problem-solving situations include the following:

- Director of manufacturing for a national steel manufacturer charged with understanding the costs associated with each stage of the highly automated, high-volume production process, so that optimal production process, product-pricing, and product-mixing strategies can be determined.
- The manager of a busy franchise in one of the leading fast-food hamburger chains must try to understand restaurant operations better in order to improve service during the hectic lunchtime rush period.
- The project manager for a famous warm-weather resort

complex is given the task of planning long-term strategy while improving short-term profits for the resort's tennis operations, which are underutilized eight months of the year and severely overcrowded during the four winter months.

- The executive vice-president of a high-volume paper manufacturer is charged with overseeing the introduction of computer technology into as many areas of the company as possible in order to increase profits and maintain the company's leadership in its field.

Obviously, POM is not just about line foremen and production machinery.

Each class discussion covers a broad array of issues. Quantitative analysis plays a very important role in POM because the numbers often do reveal where the problems are and which available solutions are economically feasible. The class quickly learns (at the expense of a few reckless Political Animals, Humanists, or Skydeckers) that it is hard to argue based on gut feeling and previous experience on Wall Street that circuit-board production should be shifted from the traditional drill press to the Modified Green Pentographic press if over seven boards or seven hundred holes are needed per order. But in one POM case study at HBS a well-executed quantitative analysis clearly won the day for the Pentographic press.

POM is also much like Marketing in that you can easily get lost in the numbers. Even when you do a thorough quantitative analysis, numbers only tell part of the story. POM teaches students that effective managers must go beyond the economics to envision what impact a change in one step of the process will have on other steps; how the change will affect the people involved; and how the change fits in with long-term corporate goals. Analysis, judgment, and sensitivity must be part of the makeup of the truly effective POM decision-maker.

POM ANALYSIS

HBS students learn as they wrestle with POM analysis that every diagram and every number represents a real machine, real work, or real workers. The analysis is only a tool that enables the manager to picture what the production process looks like, how it works, what its strengths and weaknesses are, where it is broken, and how it can be fixed or improved.

Picture the manager of a McDonald's or a Burger King restaurant as we survey the different aspects of production and operations management; we'll use the HBS case studies on these well-known competitors as illustrations throughout the chapter. In examining a business that millions of Americans can clearly picture, we'll cover the high spots of the same territory that HBS students traverse as they read a forty-page case packed with details about complicated and obscure POM environments.

In POM, as in all other HBS courses, students are taught to look first at the whole business in order to get a sense of how the company competes.

For both McDonald's and Burger King, the business is fast food. Each must produce a limited line of good-tasting products, serve its customers fast, and keep the average customer's check to about $2. To remain profitable, the company must serve a high volume of customers each day and keep those customers coming back.

Because each company is also in the franchising business, its methods must be highly standardized. Each outlet must utilize space efficiently and achieve strong quality control no matter who the manager or employees are. Consistency is a key success factor in any franchising operation.

As any fast-food gourmet knows, however, the two companies differ from one another. Burger King has always emphasized giving customers a choice of what they want on their burger; McDonald's has stressed speed and consistent quality. And Burger King has spent millions of advertising dollars telling us they "flame broil" burgers, but McDonald's fries theirs.

Keep those facts in mind as we move on to an analysis of the production and operations of each restaurant.

DRAWING A PROCESS-FLOW DIAGRAM

A simple process-flow diagram is one basic POM tool HBS students learn to master. As students read each case they try to picture in their minds and on paper the materials being used, the human or machine steps the materials go through, and the amount of time required for each step. Good diagramming is essential to turning complex, confusing production processes into a format that can be understood and analyzed.

Let's focus on McDonald's. What actually goes on in back when the manager yells to the back of the store over the sandwich bin, "Six burgers and two Macs, please?" After reading the HBS case, one is able to draw a diagram of McDonald's sandwich process that looks like the one below.

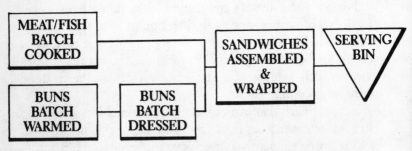

FIGURE 5–1. Flow Diagram of McDonald's Sandwich Preparation Process

Each box in a process-flow diagram represents a production step; each triangle represents an inventory of some kind. In this case, finished sandwiches in the serving bin are the ultimate goal.

When the manager shouts, an attentive grill operator hears the call, removes twelve hamburger patties from a small freezer next to the grill and lays them on the rectangular grill in two rows of six. The grill operator presses a timing switch the instant the burgers hit the grill, which is designed to hold rows of six. Grill attendants have strict instructions never to cook more than twelve patties per batch and never to have more than two batches going at one time in order to maintain quality and consistency. The operator reacts to buzzers from the timer and grills the burgers for a specified number of seconds; sears them at a specified moment; turns them at another prescribed juncture; and pulls them off the grill within a second or two of McDonald's standard. Whether one is eating a Big Mac in San Francisco, Boston, or London, it is the same size, same weight, and it has been prepared according to McDonald's precise specifications. If one enjoys the Big Mac and fries in San Francisco, odds are high they will be equally enjoyable in Boston.

While the burgers are being cooked, the buns are going through a heating and dressing process that is just as quick and well organized. Just seconds before the burgers are ready, the warm, dressed buns will be put up on a tray hooked next to the grill. The world's biggest klutz could move the burgers off the grill and onto the buns without missing.

The sandwiches are immediately wrapped in packages that preserve their warmth and identify them by type, and are slid down the appropriate chute into the serving bin near the serving counter. On either side of the sandwich bin are the other food items a customer may order—drinks, desserts, and fries. All are easily within reach of a hustling counter person. McDonald's does not encourage customers to ask for two all-beef patties, lettuce, cheese, hold the sauce, pickles, onions, hold the ketchup, on whole wheat toast. But it doesn't expect its customers to wait in line long either.

Managers watch the flow of customers and orders, and direct the flow of different sandwich types being made. As long as everyone works diligently and swiftly, the operation runs like clockwork. There just isn't much to go wrong.

Burger King evolved during the 1960s and 1970s trying to differentiate itself from its rival, which led it to employ a different production strategy; one designed to let BK tailor what the customer got on the sandwich and to give the customer a "flame-broiled" burger. It was a clear case of designing the production process to meet the company's strategic needs.

When a customer walks in and wants a Whopper with ketchup, mustard and mayo only, the production process can be diagrammed as follows.

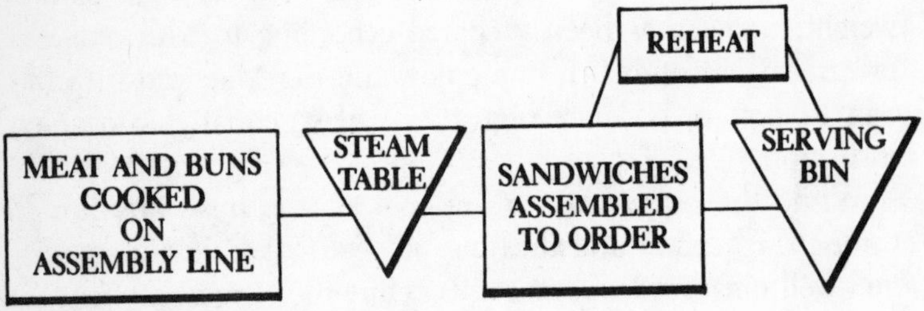

FIGURE 5–2. Flow Diagram of Burger King's Sandwich Preparation Process

Burger King's process is an assembly-line method, in contrast to McDonald's batch-cook process. A broiler operator feeds patties and buns onto a chain conveyor belt that slowly moves the patties and buns through a broiler tunnel and then deposits them in a catch bin at the end. The catch bin is on a steam table of sorts to keep the patties and buns somewhat warm.

The steam table is set next to the far end of the long stainless-steel preparation counter one sees directly ahead in the kitchen when standing at the Burger King counter. Preparers on either side of the preparation counter listen for the customer service reps at the front to call the customer's order into the microphone. One then grabs the burger and bun off the steam table, lays them on an appropriate wrapper or box taken from a shelf above the counter, dresses the sandwich according to the customer's instructions, wraps it, pops the sandwich into the microwave oven for a few seconds if that seems necessary, and slides it down the appropriate chute to the serving area (specially prepared sandwiches through one chute, standard sandwiches through another).

Every production process has certain strengths and weaknesses—one primary reason why production decisions must be tailored carefully to the needs of the business. BK's process enables it to customize sandwiches and to broil them. These features are of great value to some customers, of little value to others, and are totally worthless to still others.

The drawbacks to Burger King's process include possible delays because of the inability to speed up the broiler chain during rush periods, the need at times for microwaving, and because there is a higher likelihood that a customer won't get the sandwich that is expected. Anyone who has waited in line at Burger King for twenty minutes during rush hour, or who drives off only to find no tomato on the Whopper even though a juicy tomato slice was the main reason the car turned into Burger King instead of McDonald's that day knows the potential weaknesses of the BK system.

It is interesting that Wendy's joined the burger wars with a production system that combines certain features of its two larger rivals. A Wendy's burger is fried in a batch just as at McDonald's, then assembled in a customized manner, à la Burger King.

Lines that sometimes make Burger King's seem like the fast lane indicate that Wendy's system is by no means perfect, however.

QUANTIFYING THE FLOW DIAGRAM

After the production flow has been diagrammed and a general assessment of its strengths and possible problem areas has been made, HBS students learn to quantify the flow diagram so as to facilitate more specific analysis. This quantifying is not a process of tricky equations, but simply a matter of observing and measuring the process and its steps in order to come up with numbers that accurately describe the process. These numbers can then be analyzed to see where problems exist and how they may be fixed.

Numbers that HBS students learn to dig out of available information include the amount of time it takes a company to produce each unit of production; the maximum number of units it can produce in a given period of time (its *capacity*); the amount of time it takes for a product to pass through each step of the process (its *throughput* time); the amount of material that goes into each process to yield a unit of output (an *input-output* analysis); the total materials cost per unit; and the total labor cost per unit. Students also observe carefully in order to understand the ebb and flow of demand for products and to evaluate how well production levels match up with the schedule of demand.

With an accurate flow diagram on paper and the critical data gathered, HBS students are then ready to try to identify problem areas and search for possible solutions.

EXAMINE THE SITUATION AND DIAGNOSE THE PROBLEM

For a fast-food restaurant, having enough fresh sandwiches of the kind customers want the second they step up to the counter is a key success factor. Nothing turns customers off faster in a fast-food restaurant than having to wait in long lines and having to step aside to wait when they finally do get to the counter. What could be worse for a fast-food manager than winding the system down in the late evening, only to suffer the shock of seeing a bus load of forty starving high schoolers on a field trip come roaring up to the front door?

Certain numbers are needed to analyze just how much of a problem this situation is for McDonald's, Burger King, or Wendy's and to see which steps each can take to address its weaknesses.

If those forty teens were to roar up to the counter, how fast could McDonald's or Burger King's operations cook up enough sandwiches to calm the mob? Throughput analysis and capacity analysis provide HBS students with useful tools for analyzing this type of problem.

Quantitative analysis may tell the following story. The batch frying process used by McDonald's allows forty-eight burgers to be thrown on the grill almost instantly if two grill people are available. The whole batch is cooked in less than two minutes, by which time two prep people have heated and started preparing the rolls based on the manager's best guess of what percent should be hamburgers, cheeseburgers, or Big Macs. Wrapped sandwiches will start sliding into the serving bin within two and a half minutes; thirty-six sandwiches (figuring half will be single burgers and half Big Macs) could be up front within four and a half minutes. Meanwhile, fries have been made and Cokes poured. A minute later, another batch of burgers will be off the grill and in the process of being prepared in order to satisfy the remaining demand. The numbers show that the McDonald's batch system is well suited to turn on quickly and pump out high volumes of its standardized sandwiches.

In fact, the numbers may show that the step in the system that limits output (the *bottleneck*) is the time it takes the people manning the cash registers to serve each customer.

Quantitative analysis of the Burger King process may show a very different situation, since its burgers and buns are fed into the broiler one or two at a time on a conveyor belt. At the end of the two-minute throughput time, one or two burgers would emerge, not a whole batch, as produced at McDonald's. Preparers would then have to make each customer's sandwich, one at a time, as it came off the line. Throughput analysis would indicate that BK's forty customers would have to wait in line significantly longer than they would at McDonald's, but at Burger King they'd "have it their way."

HBS students also learn techniques that enable them to conduct overall capacity analysis and to match production capacity to demand flow—techniques that both McDonald's and Burger King managers could put to good use. Managers could chart the number of customers they expect per hour per day of the week. They then could calculate their stores' maximum capacity per hour and their capacity with different numbers of workers in order to decide whether it is necessary to expand or how best to schedule labor during the day to meet anticipated demand.

WRITE THE PRESCRIPTION

As usual, the POM manager's job has only begun when the problem has been identified. The most important part of the job is to write the correct prescription—that is, the one that solves the problem quickly, permanently, at the most reasonable cost, and with the least-negative side effects.

The numbers analysis comes in handy at this stage, enabling the manager to evaluate alternative solutions. Would a broiler assembly that pulled through more than one burger at a time be enough to meet rush-hour needs? Would three at a time be required? How much would that assembly cost? Would two separate broiler mechanisms be more efficient? And the cost of adding the second? If the capacity of the broiler is increased, how does that affect the number of preparers needed or cash registers required to be able to speedily sell the product that is ready? What would be the total cost of the desired changes?

HBS students learn, using case studies, that management's judgment, experience, and its understanding of corporate goals and sense of its operation's key success factors then come into play. The best decisions are the ones that best fit the needs of the situation after careful evaluation of all relevant factors.

Creativity also comes into play. There are countless possible solutions to any problem. Determining the best of four lousy solutions based on brilliant quantitative analysis won't build the corner hot-dog stand into the next McDonald's or Burger King.

THE SEVEN M's OF POM

There are seven major POM systems that can be examined to try to improve an operation. It's an aid to memory that each starts with the letter *M*. They are:

1. *Man- and Womanpower.* Effective management of workers is a powerful tool to improve a system's function.
2. *Materials.* The materials used can greatly affect how a process should be designed, how swiftly and efficiently it runs, and what level of product quality can be achieved.
3. *Machines.* Choosing machines with the right (for your needs) size, speed, capacity, flexibility, reliability, features, and operational capabilities is a cornerstone of good POM. Knowing when and how to incorporate new technology is an increasingly important factor in keeping a business competitive and profitable; this topic is the focus of several HBS case studies.
4. *Managers.* The quality of managers—their training and experience, and their ability to motivate workers—is an action lever POM decision-makers control through hiring and incentive practices.
5. *Messages.* Making sure the right information is communicated to the right people at the right time is also a cornerstone of a good production system. A McDonald's grill operator may be producing quarter-pounders like the wind, but if the people standing at

the register have ordered Big Macs the system has failed.

6. *Methods*. There often exist more ways than one to accomplish needed tasks. Choosing the best method for the job at hand is as important as selecting the most efficient machine or worker.

7. *Money*. Understanding the financial end of a production process and matching the system's financial needs to the corporation's needs is necessary to keep the machines running and the company profitable. A new piece of equipment may be the best long-term solution to a problem, but if the company is strapped for cash, the manager's responsibility is to find the best alternative given the funds at hand.

HBS students are taught that they must intelligently and creatively manage all seven of these POM subsystems to address the problems in the best possible manner.

THE BEST POM PRESCRIPTION

HBS students are taught to avoid making decisions based solely on the numbers. There are so many of them in most POM cases that by the time they are all crunched, it's tempting to just circle the best one and go to bed. A walk through a McDonald's kitchen, a steel mill, an auto plant, an advertising agency, or a mom-and-pop grocery store is enough to make it clear that it isn't numbers that ultimately get the product out the door. It's men and women, materials, machines, managers, messages, methods and money, all working together in some positive way.

The best classroom recommendations and exam answers are those that use the numbers but that also find the reality behind the numbers. They include recommendations that make quantitative economic sense and that also work in the mill or garage or kitchen. These are the only types of examination answers that earn students E's in POM because they are the only ones that have a chance of working in the real world.

APPRECIATING THE IMPORTANCE OF POM AND ITS STRATEGIC ROLE

HBS students are taught that strong POM decision-making and the execution of decisions are critical to the success of any business. They learn through study of real-world examples how important it is that POM decision-makers be included in the process of setting corporate goals and how important it is for POM decisions to be made in the context of the needs, strengths, and weaknesses of the entire company.

If all that seems obvious, there are times we need to take a good, hard look at the obvious. For anyone in a position to take steps, large or small, to reverse the erosion of the United States world leadership in many areas of production, especially in capital-intensive production-driven industries that produce automobiles, steel, and semiconductors, emphasis on strong POM decisions cannot be overemphasized.

THE POM CHECKLIST

To quickly evaluate a company's strengths in the production and operations management area, consider the following questions.

1. Are production and operations positions accorded a reasonable level of importance and respect?
2. Are people with the necessary skills and growth potential being encouraged to join the POM area?
3. Is someone with the knowledge of and control over the company's production and operations areas included in management decisions about corporate strategic direction?
4. Are the company's POM strategies and policies consistent with the company's overall goals and needs?

5. Is attention paid to all seven subsystems that interact to form the company's overall production system?
6. Is the company's POM system playing as much of a strategic role as it can to create sustainable competitive advantage for the company in its marketplace?

6

HUMAN RESOURCE MANAGEMENT

Although they do not show up on the balance sheet, a company's human assets are at least as important as its fixed assets—technology, cash, and raw materials. The ideas and actions of employees make the difference between a successful company and one that goes bust.

Companies such as IBM, 3M, and McDonald's have found ways to manage the relationship between the organization and its employees that ensure the organization's performance excels in both the short and long term; that offer employees economic and psychological well being; and that support the values of society. Such companies are recognized as most desirable places to work because of their attention to implementing human resource programs that attract competent people, motivate them to do a good job, and give them both intrinsic satisfaction and external rewards. The three companies named above are also leaders in their industries. Contrary to the belief that too much attention to people issues is a drag on earnings, these comon earnings, these companies are proving that there are sound economic reasons for establishing effective people-management practices as a top corporate priority.

But a great many companies still have a lot to learn about maximizing the effectiveness of their human resources. Companies have traditionally had a personnel department staffed primarily by women. Personnel was an administrative function, which involved hiring lower-level employees, cutting pay checks, and conducting exit interviews when employees left the company. For the most part, personnel policies focused on this necessary bureaucracy. The functional area managers, usually men, were too busy thinking about "real business issues," like marketing and finance, to worry about personnel matters.

Gradually, however, yesterday's personnel department has become today's human resource management (HRM) group. This represents a change in approach as well as a change in name. HRM now treats seriously the issues of how to attract, develop, and motivate people, and how to utilize them effectively.

Human Resource Management, as taught at HBS, focuses on the policies, systems, and practices put in place to govern the elements that affect employees. These include such issues as who will have a voice in HRM decisions and how that voice will be represented; how people will move into, through, and out of the organization; how they will be rewarded for their efforts; and how their work will be designed and evaluated.

The HRM course itself seemed to occupy one of the lower rungs on the academic totem pole at HBS in 1982. Some students took the course less than seriously and most left the HRM case reading and preparation to last. If a case just couldn't get read every once in a while, HRM cases tended to get the vote for loss leader. This was due in part to the fact that the material was less quantitative and easier to participate in without being thoroughly prepared. But it was also due to a relaxed, almost hesitant manner among many HRM instructors. It was as if they had not learned to flex their muscles in the HBS system.

The 1980s have become the decade in which HRM has emerged as a "real business" hot topic. Managers realize that generating profits in an environment of increasing competition depends on human resources. Changes in the work force and its demands for improved quality of life—employees are less willing to move for their job; they want more leisure time; qualified women and minorities want access to the same jobs white males have—have forced managers to become more involved in human resources. Increasing international competition, especially from Japan, where cultural norms and management practices afford relatively low labor costs; as well as increasing government intervention and the growing size and complexities of organizations is forcing U.S. managers to examine their human resource policies and procedures. Although human resource management as a serious endeavor has come about in the United States because of external pressure, it is an area of major opportunity for managers and organizations.

However, human resource management is one of the more difficult tasks required of managers. As with every decision, trade-offs exist. The trade-offs in human resource management are especially difficult to make because the consequences can be so severely felt. No longer is the issue whether business needs high quality human resource management; the issue now is how to establish it.

There is a trend in the U.S. toward increasing workers' participation in decisions about how businesses are run. Moves by all of the U.S. auto makers to increase union workers' say in shop management issues is one clear example. GM's Saturn project—its purpose is to build a new type of car—supposedly will take this trend even further.

Traditional top-down decision-making by autocratic managers has changed at some plants to a more participative decision-making process, with decisions made by the people who will be involved in implementing the plan. Heavily layered hierarchical management has become relatively flat in some organizations, with decisions being pushed to the lowest levels. In many cases the decision-implementation process has changed from top-down task assignment to management by objectives (MBO), with the objectives decided upon jointly by workers and managers.

Many managers may fear that they will lose control and power; that decisions will take more time to make; and that costs will skyrocket as workers spend more time off the "production line," involved in planning. But the potential benefits are reduced conflict, improved quality of work, and accelerated implementation of decisions and plans. The intrinsic rewards for workers that emanate from these policies may also make it easier for them to accept lesser-paying jobs.

Since 1981, HBS has been making an effort to raise future managers' awareness of human resource issues by including the Human Resource Management course in the required first-year curriculum. HBS teaches the HRM course as part of a series of human relations courses. HRM fits in after students have been exposed to the dynamics of human behavior in Organizational Behavior, Part I, and before their study of how to implement overall organizational effectiveness in OB, Part II. The HRM course is designed to teach students how to assess an organization's human resource management needs and how to establish human resource policies and procedures that are consistent with the overall corporate strategy, and that enable the organization to develop and utilize employees' capabilities effectively.

These policies should ensure a company's access to a pool of workers who are committed to the organization and good at their job, while also minimizing both the total costs paid by the organization and the potential conflict between management, employees, and the community. Through case-study analysis, students examine the opportunities, limitations, and risks associated with both traditional and innovative human resource management policies. Among the concepts that are integral to the course are employee motivation, productivity, product quality, and employee perception of management's evenhandedness. Human resource policies and procedures offer a manager highly effective vehicles for establishing positive communication with employees; indeed, a well-designed human resource program provides the manager with some of the most productive action levers.

Developing HRM policies that are consistent with other company policies is strongly emphasized throughout the HRM case discussions.

But even in this age of "enlightened" attitudes toward human resource management in the corporate world, and despite its being taught as a full-fledged course at HBS, the discipline still has a long way to go to be treated with the same level of seriousness as financial management. There are very few HBS graduates who become HRM specialists. Finance and marketing are still perceived to be more prestigious, powerful positions, and they pay better.

Students' carefree attitude toward HRM is ironic, because the subject matter embodies exactly those issues HBS graduates are most interested in for themselves when choosing a place to work: upward mobility, level and nature of compensation, amount of input into working conditions, and general work environment.

Interest in and attention to human resource management is definitely on the rise, however, and our objective in this chapter is to explain some of HBS's approaches to human resource management issues and to present a framework for thinking through human resource management issues.

THE HUMAN RESOURCE DECISION-MAKER

Every manager is a human resources decision-maker. Everyone who manages others, or even interacts with others frequently, sends signals and makes countless human resource management choices daily. The better aware people are of their decisions, the more productively decisions can be managed. Companies that rely solely on human resource departments and/or senior management to shoulder the responsibility for developing solid human resource practices are blind to the true power of the discipline.

HRM cases challenge students to deal with people-management issues from the perspective of a variety of managerial positions, including the following:

- The president of a medium-sized bank faced with potential unionization
- A middle manager directed to give a performance appraisal to an employee who has not been performing up to standard but who has never in many years at the company been told that his work is not satisfactory
- A personnel director of a manufacturing company faced with having to reduce the managerial work force by 20 percent, trying to decide how to implement the layoffs without devastating those leaving and those remaining
- The owner of a small machine shop about to enter collective-bargaining sessions with the engineering-workers union over wage and other benefit demands, faced with the unacceptable option of significant labor cost increases or a bankruptcy-threatening strike.

In many of the companies cited in the case studies, no formal corporate HRM policies had been developed to guide managers' actions. In others, companies had institutionalized human resource management guidelines.

General managers at all levels should be encouraged to suggest changes in the system for the good of the business and the employees. They should also be up to date with the policies of their competitors and other companies so they can anticipate actions in the marketplace.

Managers sensitive to human resource issues can be creative about developing ways to improve the company's ability to attract and develop the best people. General managers should have input into policies that are set because they are the ones who must implement them, and because they are the ones who know what the risks and limitations of these policies will be. Human resource specialists can be included as consultants on human resource policy, but they should never be the ultimate decision-makers.

WHAT TYPES OF DECISIONS ARE MADE

In a case examined in an HRM class, a compensation issue arose in a leading multinational company in which two important—but younger—managers in the finance division resigned to go to competitive companies for significantly higher salaries.

The head of the finance group had wanted several months earlier to pay both of them more money; he believed their performance merited the increases. But the head of human resources knew that the raised salaries would not fit within the company's established pay ranges, which were based on position, age, and experience. In addition, his annual surveys indicated that both men's salaries were already competitive with industry norms.

All hell broke loose when the two young superstars announced their resignations. Fingers pointed in all directions, and the CEO finally called in some human resource consultants to help assess the situation.

Class discussion brought to the surface how many different issues were involved in the case. Who was in charge of human resource policy was one question at issue. The head of human resources apparently refused to approve the raises, but shouldn't the finance group head ultimately be responsible for caring for his employees? The company had clearly established policies, but were they adequately tailored to meeting the company's need to keep strong performers? Should special rules be written for strong performers, or should they be let go if they disrupt the system? Was money the real reason the people left or was it just the easiest excuse?

It became clear during the class discussion that besides many problems and their possible causes, the CEO, the head of finance, and the human resource director each had their preference for how to deal with the issue. The CEO wanted to keep quality people but at the lowest possible cost. The head of finance wanted to hire and keep the superstars, paying what was necessary to keep them. The head of human resources was particularly concerned about preserving equity across the entire organization and not overreacting to turnover. This tension is common to many businesses we have been involved with and gets to the heart of many human resources decisions.

The class consensus was that compensation authority be given to the line managers, since they are the ones who best know who is performing well and who ultimately have responsibility for hiring and keeping the proper individuals.

Employees think first of their own concerns and react to the world based on their perceptions. They decide individually how they will act and produce, and only they, not the manager, can motivate themselves to do a high-quality job. They are altogether unlike the shipment of raw steel that the purchasing agent orders, knowing exactly what quality of material he's getting.

People compare their state of well-being to that of other people—within their division, the company, their town; across the country and the world. Their frame of reference goes well beyond the group in which they work. If people don't like the way they are being treated, they will naturally become less productive, or they may leave.

Equity, then, must be maintained. That's not to say that all employees in all businesses must be paid according to the same scale. Rather, all employees should perceive that the criteria used to determine how people are treated and what people are paid is fair and that those criteria are equitably applied throughout the company.

Analysis is complex, and decision-making difficult, in human resource management. But the consequences of foregone analysis and insensitive decision-making are too far-reaching and economically damaging to be tolerated.

HRM ANALYSIS AND DECISION-MAKING

HBS teaches students that when trying to solve human resource problems, they should analyze first the current conditions and their context, then the current human resource policies and the effects of those policies. Then, students are taught to lay out options in the situation; to assess the benefits and costs of each; and to choose the one most likely to achieve the desired outcome most cost effectively.

HBSers try to structure effective recommendations to take into account stakeholder influence, human resource flow, reward systems, and work systems.

ANALYZING THE BUSINESS CONTEXT

As with most other types of analysis, HBS encourages students to begin their analysis of HRM policies and practices with a thorough analysis of the business context. Students work to understand the business's key success factors and the company's goals and strategies for succeeding—knowledge that affords insight into which jobs are crucial to the company's success.

One of Texas Instrument's key success factors in calculator production over the years has been low-cost production; this has been achieved through high-volume and cost-effective production processes. For Hewlett-Packard, which competes by providing high quality and state-of-the-art features in its calculators, research and development and product innovation are key. The differences in the types of people these companies hire and reward reflect the differences in their business strategies. TI seeks out technicians who are trained to drive down production costs, while HP puts emphasis on hiring creative product-development engineers.

Another important contextual factor is the cost structure of a company. In the airline industry the salary expenses of some companies is as high as 30 percent of revenues; the ability to find ways to cut that cost affords a competitive advantage.

New York Air and People Express undercut the competition by running without the high-priced union contracts that other airlines are locked into. People Express keeps costs low and motivation high with innovative human-resource management ideas, such as giving employees equity participation in the company and enhancing their workday by broadening the types of tasks they are responsible for.

In a business such as mainframe computer sales, where salary expense is a low proportion of sales, companies have more flexibility in how they choose to reward their people.

The amount of qualified labor available is another contextual factor that affects how flexible a company can be in choosing human resource policies. The airline that wants high-quality pilots must put together a highly attractive human resource package and work hard to avoid high turnover. At the other end of the spectrum, a local service station that hires teenagers to pump gas does not need to be concerned about its human resources package or turnover rate.

The analyst's objective is to understand the company's objectives, priorities, opportunities, and constraints as well as those of the labor force, the union, the government, and other stakeholders.

SETTING HRM OBJECTIVES

To help guide the development of appropriate objectives for human resource recommendations, HBS students are taught to categorize policy objectives in four distinct areas:

Commitment. What can be done to maximize commitment to the company by the work force? Countless studies as well as common sense say that committed workers work harder and do better work. Strong commitment also minimizes hiring and training costs in many instances.

Competence. Which policies and programs are available to raise the level of worker competence? With increased competence comes improved product quality and productivity.

Cost-effectiveness. Are policies in place to increase the company's cost-effectiveness? It is obvious this factor is a major concern to all companies, but it is especially critical to those companies facing stiff competition and tight profits. However, cost-effectiveness does not always result from cutting salaries or reducing benefits. In many instances, paying higher salaries or increasing benefits can lead to efficiency increases. Many investment banks and consulting firms have found that paying lucrative salaries is the way to attract and keep the people who set profits climbing.

Congruence. Are there ways to bring the values and expectations of all parties involved more into line with one another? Minimizing conflicts between worker and manager, company and family, or company and the community is often smart business. Keeping human resource policies consistent with one another and with company goals is also part of this policy objective.

The HBSer who has analyzed the context and established the key objectives demanded by the situation is then ready to begin identifying human-resource management options and recommendations, selecting from among the range of managerial action levers available.

DEVELOPING HRM RECOMMENDATIONS— FOUR KEY AREAS OF CONCENTRATION

HBS students learn to put their recommendations into four categories in order to make sense out of often complex options. These categories are broad, but enable the student to identify distinct avenues by which managers' decisions and policies affect a company's human resources.

STAKEHOLDER INFLUENCE

Systems and practices put in place by management with regard to stakeholder influence determine which employees perceive themselves as having a voice in governing the organization.

These systems and practices also determine the methods by which different groups participate in governing the firm, and the procedures for resolving conflicts of interest. The primary stakeholders include management, employees, union leaders, owners, suppliers, customers, and the government. Each stakeholder has its own interests and is in search of a way to express its ideas and defend its needs.

HBS students consider many types of policy decisions dealing with stakeholder interests. Management can solicit stakeholder ideas or simply react to them when they surface. Soliciting ideas often elicits cooperation and commitment, and may also produce information about issues of concern to the organization before they become costly problems. A management that is primarily reactive may be blindsided by issues.

There are certain issues that management would like to examine in an open forum, and others that it would like to deal with quietly. Some managers feel all issues should be open for debate. Increased openness has strong benefits as long as management is flexible enough to deal with issues that may arise and workers are reasonable in their requests.

Managers must decide which vehicles will be established to allow stakeholders to be heard on issues of interest. These vehicles include meetings, surveys, lunches with management, open-door policies; as well as vehicles that give employees access to employee-relations representatives, union grievance procedures, and even worker representatives on the board of directors.

A typical management fear is that if stakeholders—particularly the workers—have too strong a voice, chaos will ensue. And that may happen if employees have a narrow, self-serving perspective with no commitment to the broader concerns of running the company. But shutting down communication is hardly a solution; the more positive challenge is to develop employees' commitment. The trend toward employee stock ownership programs is one step in the drive to build commitment to the company through employee involvement.

An argument managers make minimizing the amount of

time they spend listening to employees and other stakeholders is that listening costs time and money and is not productive. The hole in that logic is that there are hidden but sizable costs related to low employee commitment. Also, employees who feel they're not being listened to may feel driven to seek a stronger voice by inviting such other potential stakeholders as unions or government to get involved.

Management in the United States inadvertently fostered the unionization movement during the industrial boom after World War II by imposing top-down decision-making and not listening to the needs, desires, and ideas of the workers on the production line.

The challenge for management remains one of maximizing stakeholder influence in ways that are cost-effective and productive. In their dealings with workers, managers must be particularly careful not to raise expectations that cannot be satisfied.

HUMAN RESOURCE FLOW

A second area of human resource decision-making is the flow of people into, through, and out of the organization—this involves recruiting, training, career counseling; as well as establishing programs and policies regarding performance assessment, job paths, promotion policies, and termination policies. Decisions made on these matters determine the quality and quantity of the labor force and also have a strong impact on employee interest in their work and commitment to the company.

Flow policies are important in all stages of a company's evolution. Fast-growing companies are constantly short of qualified staff. Stable companies are challenged to find ways to meet their promise to promote people when higher level positions are not being vacated. Companies in decline often must make major decisions about how to shrink the work force.

The decision by AT&T, in August 1985, to shrink some of its operations by 20,000 people put a massive burden on the company, the employees, their families, and society, which must support those who are unemployed or absorb them into other businesses, sometimes with retraining.

Who will be promoted? Who will go for career development workshops? Who will be terminated? Flow policies must be perceived as fair.

Many organizations have found that the best way to foster equity—as well as the perception that policies are equitable— is to have an objective performance-appraisal system that is used systemically by all managers with all employees. Corporations must decide who will do the appraisals, how often, and on what criteria they will be based. The corporation must also determine what career paths should look like, and who it is that decides which individuals will take which path based on which criteria. Multiple career tracks and job posting give people a feeling of freedom of choice and can help reduce turnover: Employees don't feel that they have to leave the company in order to advance. In one policy option, employees are moved laterally to learn a new skill once a given job has been mastered—a program many companies have had a hard time implementing because American culture places such a high value on quick upward mobility.

Recruiting is where the flow starts. Guidelines must be related to job designs and rewards. Hiring the right person for the organization is crucial for reducing unnecessary turnover and for getting work done well and at the right price.

Recruiters must be intimately familiar with the job skills for each position they recruit for; with the type of culture that exists within the organization; and with the traits that are likely to lead to success in the organization. They should also be able to extract meaningful information from candidates about their skills and potential fit in the organization. The quality and status of those sent to recruit is a strong signal to job seekers about the importance the company puts on human resource issues.

Other issues that should be considered regarding the human resource flow are what the optimal turnover rate is in the business, whether an "up or out" policy makes sense in the business, whether the company should help place the people it terminates in other jobs, and whether career counseling is a valuable investment.

REWARD SYSTEMS

Reward system policies focus on salaries, bonuses, merit increases, perquisites, fringe benefits, awarding of titles, and a myriad of other noneconomic rewards available to managers to help them communicate with, direct, and motivate their employees. Reward decisions affect the quality of work, the cost of work, employee morale, and the sense of equity within the organization.

The mix of economic and noneconomic rewards available to employees is designed to motivate them to do what is good for the organization by doing what is good for themselves; reward systems should make the goals of the individual congruent with the goals of the organization in the most cost-effective way possible. Thus, the mix of rewards must take into account both what the results of the job should be and what it is that motivates the employee doing the job. For example, in an environment where many leads for new-product sales could come through referrals from the service side of the operation, as in a luxury car dealership, managers may want to consider paying service people for qualified sales leads, or rewarding them with extra time off.

Effective reward systems don't have to be expensive. One of the ways to make the rewards most cost-effective is to maximize the noneconomic rewards that people get from doing the job. One of the ways for companies to do this is to hire people who will enjoy and get satisfaction out of the tasks required. Another is to build a winning team that people are proud to be associated with. Or, tasks can be designed so that employees can see a whole project through from start to finish. Many auto manufacturers are doing this with work teams that build a whole portion of a car or truck, rather than having each person do one isolated task on an assembly line. Giving someone a career-enhancing responsibility can be a reward that costs almost nothing.

United States companies have traditionally rewarded people with bonuses and promotions; with status symbols, such as a corner office; and with salaries based on a job to be done. However, problems arise if the market value of a person's skills far exceeds the pay received but corporate guidelines prohibit raises; or if bonuses are paid that do not seem to be tied directly to performance. When economic incentives alone are counted on to maintain worker motivation, the company risks losing its best employees to any competitor with deeper pockets.

A more participatory approach would involve paying people enough to attract and keep them based on their skills; allowing peer groups some voice in who should get promoted to a job position that becomes available; minimizing the number of status symbols in order to foster a sense of teamwork; and tying incentive pay directly to performance measures.

Whatever rewards are decided upon, it is important that they constantly be adjusted to reflect changes in the work force, jobs, and in business conditions in order to maintain a reward program with the correct strategic fit.

WORK SYSTEMS

Work systems, the final decision-making area, include such matters as job structuring, segmenting the labor force, identifying the points at which decisions are made and who it is that makes them, choosing methods for evaluating performance, and determining who reports to whom in the workplace.

American blue-collar and clerical workers have traditionally been given simple, repetitive tasks to do under close supervision. Performance over the years would indicate that little commitment to the organization or the quality of work is engendered. However, production does go on.

A more participatory style of management, such as that touted by GM's Saturn project, and as practiced by the Japanese, assigns teams to get a particular product made and helps them feel more self-directed in their work. Job assignments are flexible, and are controlled by the team, perhaps with an advisor. The team is ultimately responsible for meeting deadlines and for managing itself. With this all-hands-on system, GM has reduced absenteeism, grievances, and cost overruns; and it has increased product quality in many of its production areas. HBS students learn that it's essential to study and improve work systems throughout the company if an attitude of cooperation is to be turned into notably improved corporate performance.

AN HRM CLASS DISCUSSION

No matter how logical and simple the HRM concepts appear to be, human resource issues are invariably complex—as class discussions proved time after time.

The following class discussion illustrates the kind of thinking process students go through to solve a human-resource management problem faced by a Japanese steel company.

"I don't understand what the issue is here. It seems perfectly obvious to me that Nippon Steel Corporation (NSC) can't afford to increase the retirement age from fifty-five to sixty, as the Japanese government has done in its country, and the union wants the company to do," said one of the Quantitative Analysis Jocks to open an HRM class. "According to my calculations, due to slackened demand, the company already has over three thousand excess employees—10 percent of the work force. That's eating up the bottom line. By increasing the retirement age, seven thousand more excess people will have to be carried by the company over the next five years."

Hands shot up in a flash. As usual, the "opener" was surrounded by people who wanted to pour light through the holes in his logic. He cringed and sat back for the onslaught.

The next student called on added qualitative perspective to the situation.

"We should step back here and examine the dynamics of the situation before coming to such a rash judgment," he said. "First, let's look at the conditions at the time of the decision. Demand for steel has historically been very strong, but has declined over the past two years. In this environment, NSC's business strategy, which has made them the world leader in steel production, has been to cut labor costs by transferring existing workers to the new jobs that arise as old ones become obsolete. This strategy has helped reduce their hiring needs and layoffs at the same time.

"In addition, the company is perceived by society as a progressive employer. That's key to industrial growth, since this is a society that values the group over the individual. Although the government is reducing its involvement, it has historically subsidized the company and the industry. Union–management relations have been cooperative; workers have gained benefits without striking. The Japanese banks are also strongly tied into NSC; they finance virtually 100 percent of the operation. Retirement age is now fifty-five. But life expectancy is increasing and workers can't afford to retire so early anymore.

"Second, look at the current human resource policies. They are appropriate in the context of the steel business; and they are consistent with each other and with social values. There are many stakeholders involved here who participate in decisions. Management wants to keep peace with labor, decrease the labor force, and manage the decline in the steel industry responsibly so as to maintain industry leadership and profits in the long run. Management has worked with the workers and unions to develop working conditions optimal for all. They have always presented decisions to the employees with all the relevant facts.

"The union wants to increase the retirement age to sixty, avoid a strike, and maintain a strong overall human resources program. The union leaders also want to maintain their moderate stance, which has brought the workers major benefits without striking.

"The workers are given a strong voice in how the processes in the business will work through self-management teams, similar to what we refer to as quality circles. They want to keep their jobs and good working conditions, and they want to increase the required retirement age.

"The government also wants to up the retirement age, to avoid social security. And it recognizes steel as a key to industrial growth.

"The human-resource flow policies and procedures have also fit with the contextual conditions up to this point. Life-long employment has been offered. This investment in the employees allows the company to give slow promotions, which, with strong training and development, ensures knowledgeable people at every level who can easily be moved laterally to perform a new task. Employee transfers are common if work loads and needs shift. The company invests in the employees and vice versa.

"The reward system has supported the flow policies. With the company paying by seniority, there's always been incentive for the employees to be loyal to the firm. And extrinsic rewards have not been the only rewards.

"The work systems have reflected the assumption that intrinsic rewards of the job are extremely important. Job descriptions have been informal and flexible, with few job levels. Decision-making has been done at the lowest possible level. Second-level managers have developed and evaluated the workers, and first-level managers and the third-level managers have developed business strategies and dealt with the banks and the government.

"After hours, self-management groups of blue collar workers have developed the process and safety improvements.

"Third, we have to look at the outcomes of these policies up to now. The mix of human resources policies has resulted in low-cost, high-quality products and innovative thinking, low employee turnover, employee commitment to the firm, and competent workers who demand only moderate wage increases and contribute annual cost reductions equal to 20 percent of employment costs through self-management groups. Employees have gained self-esteem and security. Society has gained a business that is a driving force in the economy.

"It seems to me that these guys have a good thing going here. The shift in demographics to a proportionately older work force and society and the decline in the demand for steel is forcing a shift in HR policies. Yes, overmanning is expensive. But profits are not critical given the financial support banks provide. A confrontation with labor could be detrimental to all parties.

"In order to maintain worldwide cost leadership, what is critical is to minimize labor costs while maintaining productivity. Maybe they should raise the retirement age, live with the cost of the excess workers and strive very hard to find ways to cut future hiring. This would fit with their strategy and traditional success factors in the industry."

A woman across the room from this long-winded "second opener," or counterpoint, had been restless, and now she jumped in.

"I agree with you in principle, now that I finally know what your point is. One way they could buy time for innovative problem-solving is not to begin to implement the new retirement age for a year."

"But," countered a man to her left, "the longer-run issue that is still unresolved with this solution is the medium-term effect on the work force—it will tend to become skewed toward the older range, the highest-paid workers under the reward system based on seniority. And fewer people being recruited will mean fewer fresh ideas."

The Skydecker in the center section allowed as how tradeoffs would have to be made on any plan that was pursued. He then added that the manner of implementation of the elected plan was critical to its success. "I think that the decision should be made through the process already in place in their traditional bottom-up manner," he said. "Then the final decisions should be presented, as usual, giving all of the facts of the situation. That cooperation between the employees and management is an asset too valuable to jeopardize."

After several hours (per student) of reading and analyzing and eighty minutes of spirited classroom debate, it was clear that many issues remained unresolved and that many more had been left untouched. As in many other classes, some students left the room distressed that more wasn't achieved. Others departed exhilarated that they had been exposed to so many issues and ideas in so short a time.

Though not a formula for solving human resource management problems, the procedures for analyzing context, laying out objectives, and focusing on recommendations in the areas of stakeholder influence, human resource flow, reward system, and work systems help HBS students know where to start asking questions and how to start thinking about possible solutions.

HBS stresses to its students in each of the first-year courses that when all of the complexities are analyzed and the necessary trade-offs made, their goal as managers is to urge that policies be consistent with one another and with the organization's objectives.

As a final example—polar to the Japanese ethos—it is instructive to look at how the most successful investment banks have put together a simple but effective human resource program in their securities trading operations. The business requires intelligent individuals working at a frantic pace, under intense pressure, in order to be profitable. Those companies hire aggressive, persistent people who are driven by one primary goal—to get rich. They pay on a full-commission basis and award huge monetary bonuses for exceeding individual quotas.

There are few frills. Traders sit at a three-foot-square maze of phones and computer screens for eight hours each day, five days a week. But good traders make $100,000 to $500,000 a year very early in their careers. Although that sounds like a high compensation cost for the companies to pay, it's worth it to them, because the top performers keep the business successful. The best people have the incentive they require to stay on. Those traders who don't bring in the business don't make enough money to keep themselves happy, and get out of the business.

Burnout and turnover are high in this pressure-cooker environment. But the supply of qualified people so exceeds demand for them that the firms are not hurt; they can inject new blood, as needed, into the system—and keep current traders on their toes.

Investment banks have found that what may seem to be a high pay scale is actually a cost-effective way to run the business in the long run. After a year of HRM case studies, HBS students are convinced that effective managers perceive human resource policies and practices as strategic choices that can make a difference in business performance. HBS teaches that the success of the human resource program should ultimately be measured by its contribution to the long-run viability and success of the business and its contribution to employees' and society's well-being.

HRM CHECKLIST

Among the key questions to be asked when assessing human-resource management thinking are the following:

1. Is someone in a position of responsibility in charge of developing overall human resource policies for the company?
2. Does that individual have access to and the full support of the company's top management?
3. Are all managers throughout the company encouraged to make effective human resource decisions and to make improvements in HR policy and practice?
4. Do the company's human resource policies foster congruence between employee wants and company needs? Do they work to foster commitment to the company, strong job satisfaction, and excellent job performance?
5. Have the areas of stakeholder influence, human resource flow, reward systems, and work systems all been addressed by management?
6. Are human resource policies constantly reevaluated to assure effectiveness?
7. Do current human resource policies foster a sense of equity in all areas of the company?

7

CONTROL

So far, we have reviewed HBS courses that deal with setting overall corporate objectives, designing an effective corporate structure, and setting strategies in functional areas of the organization. In this chapter, we will examine how a company monitors and communicates its programs—how it keeps score.

Control is the Harvard Business School first-year course that shows MBA students how to keep a corporate scorecard and how to interpret effectively the information on it. The course teaches the development and use of accounting systems to measure financial performance management; information and control systems to track performance in relation to objectives; and financial reporting systems to communicate performance. The tools students learn to use in the Control course are applied to responsibility center assignment, establishment of transfer prices, budget development, variance analysis, and financial statement analysis. Accounting tools are also used in the control process.

The emphasis is on interpretation and decision-making. Cases and class discussions demonstrate that effective managers understand which variables must be measured in order to track company performance with the greatest accuracy; how numbers must be applied in order to direct and motivate people to meet their objectives; and how the organization's performance must be communicated in order to convey management's intended messages to all relevant stakeholders.

The controller, as seen by HBS, is more than a high-level accountant, but rather a strategist and decision-maker who specializes in obtaining, interpreting, and communicating data on corporate performance. Working closely with senior managers from all areas of the company, the controller is responsible for checking the corporate navigation instruments that keep the business on track; and for recognizing when and to what extent the business has wandered off track so that the deviation can be corrected.

It is not surprising that this perspective on the control function thrilled HBSers with accounting backgrounds who knew the power of their craft. Most of us without an accounting background were shocked that the discipline had so much potential impact on management. A surprising number of students actually grew to enjoy the course even though they were not accountants or Quantitative Analysis Jocks. Although at first blush Control is a "hard" course, it fits closely with OB, HRM, and Management Communications.

That's not to say that the cases don't call for plenty of number crunching. As expected, the CPAs and bankers found the quantitative techniques a relative breeze, and many in our class tutored their classmates. One of the key success factors in forming a study group, which many of us didn't figure out until it was too late, is to get someone with a financial background into your group to help do the legwork in Control.

These four fundamental questions are examined from a variety of managerial perspectives in Control:

1. How has the organization done in the past?

2. How will it do in the future?
3. How can management measure performance against its objectives and help ensure the organization's future success?
4. How should management communicate this performance to stakeholders, both inside and outside the organization?

During our time at HBS, the guts of financial accounting techniques were covered in the first month of classes. Although this was a new language and a new way of thinking for most of us, HBS assumed we would pick up the accounting mechanics on our own by pondering our notes, reading textbooks, analyzing cases, and staying alert in class discussions. Most class time was spent arguing the interpretation of the accounting, not reviewing the mechanical techniques. That emphasis appealed to many of us who were much better at arguing with classmates than balancing debits and credits; but it was not uncommon for a class to go by in which the "hard" analysis was discussed only by the six or eight people with an accounting background, while those without a financial background tried to chime in with relevant comments on the company's strategy objectives and management background just to get air time in this course, much of the content of which was going right over their heads. In the inimitable HBS way, though, we did learn simultaneously (if with varying degrees of comprehension) both how to use the analytic techniques and how to interpret the results.

Study of management control systems during the second half of the course was a welcome change for most, since it required less technical analysis. But it too brought frustrations, because there was never a "right" answer as there had been in the accounting portion. We never did decide what the optimal transfer price was. It was an issue of continual controversy and much confusion, reminiscent of the debate over weighted average cost of capital debated in Finance.

Those who thrived on control issues looked forward to a

number of in-depth, second-year Control courses, such as Advanced Cost Accounting, Analysis of Corporate Financial Reports, Cost Analysis and Control, and Managing for Control. Other HBSers made a note to avoid those very courses.

Like HBS, this chapter will focus more intensely on how to interpret and use financial information than on how to develop it. Our objective is to relay our interpretation of the issues stressed in the HBS Control course so that one could apply the information to specific business situations.

WHO IS THE DECISION-MAKER?

A man who was getting ready to retire from his business had no one to turn it over to. He went looking for the next CEO of the company and narrowed his choice to his senior engineer, his senior research scientist (a mathematician) and his controller.

He thought of one question to ask each to see who gave the best answer, and called them into his office one by one.

First, the senior engineer came in. The businessman said, "Warren, what does one and one equal?" Warren, having spent a lifetime working with binary numbers, said, "one and one is 10."

Next, the old man called in his senior scientist. "Sharon," he asked, "what is one and one?" Sharon, having received all of her degrees from MIT, stated, "one and one is one prime."

Finally, the man called in the company's controller. "Dan, I've asked Warren and Sharon this question, and frankly, I'm not sure I like their answers. Tell me, Dan, what is one and one?" Dan took off his glasses, put his arm around the man's shoulder and said, "Tell me, boss, what do you want it to be?"

Dan was probably an outstanding controller and most likely an HBS graduate.

As the tale illustrates, control decisions should be a joint effort between the controller and other senior managers and business managers in the organization. The implications of the controller's decisions are far-reaching and should be made in conjunction with all of the other business decisions. Then, they must be fully communicated to a number of interested parties.

On the outside looking in, there are creditors, investors, potential creditors and investors, as well as competitors, who are extremely interested in the financial performance of the company. Many of them have analysts whose job it is to dig into companies' financials to understand how well they are performing and why.

In the HBS Control class, students are asked to look at the world as seen by individuals in some of the following positions:

- A member of the board of directors of an airline contemplating a change in the content and form of information reported to the public and deciding if it should include a statement of changes in financial position
- A general manager trying to decide what kind of budgeting process he should use, how it should be tied to strategic planning, and who should be involved in the process
- A securities analyst making a recommendation about whether or not to put a major proprietary hospital on the "buy list."

The primary role of the controller, together with general managers, and outside financial analysts, is to develop and interpret financial information, and to provide analysis of that information that is useful for decision-making purposes. Such information should highlight the appropriate issues in a given situation; it should be timely, accurate, and presented in a form that can be acted on. Information that fails to meet even one of these criteria can be worthless, sometimes even harmful.

The controller is responsible for tracking performance and providing the general managers of business units with timely and specific information about performance results, about the cause of those results, and about projections for the future. In addition to being the person tracking the course of the corporate ship, the controller must make sure the ship has the proper instruments for measuring its progress—all the informational tools a ship's captain and crew must have to maximize their performance. The controller must often develop those instruments specifically to suit a particular business. In a company, the instruments would be part of the management information systems (MIS) and the management control systems (MCS).

The controller must have a sound knowledge of the objectives and strategy of the business as well as its day-to-day operations in order to understand how to measure business variables and their significance for the company's overall success.

It may be necessary or advantageous for the organization to keep different sets of books for each of the different constituencies. It is up to the controller, along with the general managers, financial officers, and communications officers to devise the appropriate information content and presentation format for each audience in order to give the correct answer to "what is one and one?"—that is, the answer that tells the audience what it needs to know about the business depending on the perspective from which the audience likes to view the business.

The controller should work closely with the operating managers, the general managers of the business units, the accounting department, the CFO, and the corporate communications department. The controller needs to have strong interpersonal skills, knowledge of human and organizational behavior, and quantitative skills, coupled with a solid understanding of the specific business in which the company is involved—the marketplace, competition, risks, and the company's strengths and weaknesses.

TYPES OF CONTROL DECISIONS

Control is all about measuring and interpreting economic reality using financial measurements. From the company's perspective, it is a way to collect information that helps managers better understand their business and better decide what actions need to be recommended. From the perspective of the outsider, such as an investor or creditor, the ability to analyze the numbers that measure corporate performance means one can gain meaningful insight into how the company may perform in the future. There are often key distinctions made between the information that is needed to manage and what is reported to outsiders.

A crucial point that HBS gets across to its students is that in order to really understand what the financial numbers mean, one must understand what they actually measure and what the underlying causes are for the numbers being what they are. Managers must be certain to measure the appropriate events and to interpret them correctly in order to gain control over the business and send the appropriate messages to the outside world—a world they depend on for financial and customer support.

The types of decisions the controller and general managers have to make regarding control issues relate directly to the four fundamental questions raised earlier:

1. How has the organization done in the past? Which portions of the company have performed well? Which poorly? What implications should be drawn?

2. How will the organization do in the future? How can estimates of future performance be made and quantified? What opportunities or problems can be identified?

3. How can management measure performance against its objectives and help to ensure the organization's future success? Which types of budgeting and cost-accounting systems make sense? Which types of management control systems make sense? Which manager should participate in this system?

4. How should management communicate performance to the outside world? What should the accounting policies be? Which format should the reporting be in? In areas where management has a choice, should the numbers reported be optimistic or conservative?

A dramatic example of an industry being forced by competitive pressures to develop better information-gathering systems is the banking industry. Prior to deregulation, most banks maintained comfortable profits by collecting cheap deposits and building solid-margin loan portfolios. To keep customers happy, they also offered them many other services at little or no charge. The control issues were of little concern during those happy days of steadily rising revenues and profits.

Deregulation has dramatically changed this situation. Bank managers now find themselves facing stepped-up competition on every front in which they do business. As competition squeezes profits in traditional areas, bank managers must reexamine all their business lines to determine current earnings and expenses and what potential for profits exists so that effective strategies can be set for the future.

A major problem has been lack of accurate information on which actions can be based. Banks need to know if there is money to be made in large corporate lending, middle-market lending, and in retail banking; what fees should be charged for checking and NOW accounts, merger and acquisition services, and mortgage refinancing services. Such questions cannot be answered properly without a tremendous amount of information many banks have never felt the need to collect. Over the past five years new managers and high-priced consulting firms have helped address these management-information system deficiencies.

ANALYTIC TECHNIQUES IN CONTROL

THE INSTRUMENTS OF MEASURE

The primary tools a controller uses to measure financial performance are variations on the standard income statement and balance sheet. The income statement reflects the flow of revenues and expenses that have occurred during the period being measured. The balance sheet reflects the values of the assets, liabilities, and equity at the end of the period. A well-thought-out control system is designed for the users of the information, so that the information they receive is meaningful and easy to read, interpret, and act upon.

The challenges are many. First, the controller must be sure that the systems designed for collecting the data measure the revenues, expenses, assets, and liabilities in a manner that is meaningful to each of the audiences who make decisions based on the statements. The controller should also see to it that the statements designed for reporting the data are reporting all, yet *only*, the necessary information required for each audience to analyze performance effectively. For instance, the executive vice-president of operations would likely be interested in analyzing performance only by department; but each department head needs performance numbers by shift.

The controller setting about to measure performance must first have a game plan for each organizational unit. This requires thinking about what the performance of each unit should be in order to see how the goals of the entire organization can be met. The needs of each unit must be known in order to determine what resources are needed by the organization and how those resources should be allocated.

The controller's game plan, reflecting sound management practice, establishes systems that encourage the people in each of the units to act in a way that helps the company meet its goals. These systems are called *management control systems*.

One type of management control system is a budget. By setting up a budget for the upcoming period, managers are forced to look beyond their day-to-day problems. The budget enables managers to set up goal and decision-making guidelines. When done well, a budget helps to ensure congruent goals for all employees and business units of the company; the budget is a particularly effective tool when it is tied in with the reward systems and the strategic planning process.

To achieve all its ends, the budget must be congruent with the business environment, the organizational structure, and the company's objectives and strategy. The way the budget is put together—the items it measures, the results it projects—all communicate expectations that senior management has for each organizational unit.

The scorecard a golfer takes onto the course gives the distance to the hole and tells what par is—how many shots it should take to get the ball in the hole. It summarizes what is being measured and what the golfer's goal is for the particular hole. In a similar manner, tallying the corporate scorecard is inextricably tied to setting the game plan, because each unit's success is judged against the expectations initially set—the par.

To know what type of budget should be put in place for each unit, the controller and general managers should first ask what part each unit should play in the company's reaching its overall goals. The answers will determine whether each unit should be a cost center or a profit center, and what type of budget objectives should be set in order to motivate the people in each unit to act in the best interest of the company.

AN HBS CASE

This typical HBS case helps illustrate the types of issues that should be considered before establishing budget figures for operating units.

A manufacturing company with high fixed costs wants to increase its market share to expand volume during a period of excess capacity. The company gives its sales force responsibility for meeting an absolute-dollar profit-contribution budget target of actual sales minus standard variable costs. Sales people may adjust the selling prices as they see fit. They are given the leeway to "buy" market share by reducing price, but are held responsible for meeting absolute-dollar contribution levels.

In other words, their incentive is to maximize the absolute amount of money available to the company to cover the fixed costs of overhead, even if it means lowering the market price to increase sales volume and revenues.

The production department, whose job it is to minimize

costs, is made a cost center. Its goal is to meet a reduced actual variable cost-per-unit target figure and a reduced overall fixed-cost target.

In our discussion of this case, an astute Skydecker noted that this production budget tempts the manufacturing department to cut the quality of the product in order to cut costs. Heads nodded. Her alternative suggestion was to make the production unit a center of profit, not cost. Its goal would be to maximize its revenues minus costs. Revenues would be generated by giving production revenue credit for each product sold. The costs subtracted from this amount would be the actual production costs, variable and fixed, accrued during the period of excess capacity. This, she suggested, would give the production unit incentive to minimize the variable as well as the fixed production costs while also maintaining the necessary quality needed to generate strong sales of the product in the marketplace. At this point, some heads were nodding and some were shaking. More than a few people looked confused. The need to assure maintained quality standards was clearly correct, but was the proposed solution on target?

A Humanist from across the room jumped on this idea with the comment, "It isn't good management to make the head of production responsible for sales unit volume, which he ultimately cannot control." A good point.

A Synthesizer from the center section noted that, assuming the criticisms of both systems are valid, and knowing there are always trade-offs in designing budget systems, it is the controller's job to analyze the results at the end of the period using the concept of a flex budget.

The underlying idea of a flex budget is to break down all the budget and actual figures—revenue and expenses—for each operating unit into component parts in order to understand which components caused the actual results to vary from the budget. The process is called *variance analysis*.

Using the current example, we can see what the controller may learn using variance analysis.

Let's assume he found that the sales force's actual profit

contribution was below target. By dissecting the sales figures into the components of total market size and total market share, and price per unit, the controller could see that the sales volume goal was not realized and that there was a volume variance. But further analysis showed that there was a 5 percent increase in market share. The overall market actually shrank by 20 percent.

The controller might have concluded then that the sales force had done a terrific job under the circumstances. The sharply declining market would be cause for concern, however, so he might decide to call an urgent meeting with the general manager and the heads of sales, marketing, production, and finance to make them aware of the change in market conditions and to begin discussion of an appropriate company response.

Let's also assume that by analyzing the manufacturing budget, he found that even if the sales force had sold the budgeted number of units, the manufacturing profits would have been below budget because actual variable costs per unit were above expectations due to labor costs. Therefore, a rate variance existed. Suppose he then pointed that out to the production manager, who discovered that the company had a new supervisor on the job who had mistakenly allowed overtime for the workers—something a more senior supervisor would not have done. Some workers who had wanted the extra pay had been performing below standard during regular hours and finishing their work on overtime at time-and-one-half pay. The production manager would now easily be able to straighten the situation out.

One can see how by sensitively breaking the budget into more manageable parts a manager can produce better information that can lead to solving problems quickly and without needless confusion or wheel-spinning.

Back in the classroom, a hand tentatively crept up in the very front row.

"If the company needs to price its products at the level of total costs, including variable and fixed costs, in order to break even, why should it not make the sales force responsible for covering both variable and fixed costs instead of just variable costs?" asked one of the Eccentrics.

Dead silence hit the class, and many pairs of eyes stared at the case in front of them or at one of the former accountants in the room. The questioner smiled slightly; perhaps he was not as dumb as he had thought.

One of the former accountants explained that volume was what the company needed to fill excess capacity, and that every unit sold above its variable cost contributed to help cover fixed costs. It was appropriate that the sales force's budget gave the salespeople incentives to make every possible sale that could be made over variable direct costs with as high a profit margin as possible. Their incentives were thus perfectly matched to the company's needs. If the salespeople felt that every sale had to cover fixed costs as well, some sales might not be made and needed contribution would be lost. Yes, the company was taking a short-term approach because in the long run, total cost per unit, which included both variable cost and fixed cost, would have to be covered in the average unit price to maintain profitability. But the company was in a short-term survival mode at this particular time and it was appropriate to offer short-term incentives.

Another CPA who was looking for air time played off this comment with her knowledge of cost accounting and cost allocation techniques. She noted that this company, by using the standard direct method of cost accounting, obtained appropriate managerial information. She added a caveat: With this accounting method, as long as standard production costs (the average cost per unit that would typically be expected if all went as planned) were set at a reasonable and appropriate level, any variance from the standard costs would be expensed as a separate line item below the gross profit line on the income statement that managers would see. That only direct (variable) production costs were assigned to each unit produced meant that fixed costs were recognized in the period in which they were incurred. Thus, they would be a visible expense to management as a line item on the income statement.

Under another method of cost accounting—the full-cost method—the company could inflate its profits by producing more units than it sold, allocating the fixed costs across all of the production units, but then expensing on the income statement only the fixed costs allocated to the fewer numbers of units sold. This method is, in fact, required for public disclosure purposes. The unrecognized portion of the fixed costs would end up sitting in the accumulated inventory on the balance sheet, making inventory look high. If an unsuspecting analyst saw the high inventory level and low level of costs reflected, respectively, in an increased current ratio and in improved profit margins, he might assume the company's liquidity and financial strength were improving. In fact, to the contrary, the company overproduced and may well have unsalable inventory on its hands in a declining industry.

As we can see, there are many ways to tally the scorecard.

The decisions about which statistics and performance results to report to whom and how to do it are up to management as long as it acts within the Securities and Exchange Commission guidelines for public information reported by public companies. Accounting policies should be and are chosen extremely carefully by senior management. They communicate as much about a company's strategy and management intentions as any other public statement, and they probably garner much closer scrutiny.

HBSers become aware that management has considerable flexibility in the numbers it reports. A new CEO coming in to turn a problem company around may choose to use the most conservative accounting policies possible to take a one-time writedown of many of the probably uncollectible receivables and much of the unsalable inventory in order to take the hits to the bottom line early in his tenure and blame the problems on his predecessor. Then he could clean house and improve the quality of future earnings by bringing the reported income closer to the actual cash being generated by operations. That's a strategy frequently used to gain investor and creditor confidence—confidence that, in itself, can help turn the business around.

On the other hand, in a company using more liberal accounting policies there is likely to be a larger discrepancy between both reported income and asset value and cash. The demise of W.T. Grant was a surprise to many major lenders who took confidence in rising net income but did not look deeply enough to realize that the company was running out of cash.

Many of the recent bank failures across the country were not anticipated because the banks did not account realistically for the high probability that many of their risky loans would never be repaid. By not writing down the value of their loans, they overstated the actual cash value of those assets.

The more HBS students learn about the mysteries embedded in accounting numbers, the more skeptical they get about "back of the envelope" financial analysis and a one-line statement in the corporate earnings section of the newspaper suggesting that, say, Wang was healthier than its major competitors because it was the only computer manufacturer to report a profit last quarter. Students find that meaningful analysis of economic reality requires knowing the business and dissecting the accounting numbers to evaluate an organization's true financial health.

The disclosure format managers choose for each audience is also flexible. For years, General Electric used a Statement of Change in Financial Position (SCFP) that highlighted its increasing working capital position. This led investors and creditors to infer that GE's liquidity was improving despite the fact that GE was actually borrowing to pay dividends. Then, in 1975, GE's working capital level declined, but its cash balances plus marketable securities increased. The company then changed its SCFP to focus on the level of these cash equivalents in an effort to keep investor confidence up.

UNDERSTANDING ECONOMIC REALITY

When trying to understand the economic reality that the financial numbers represent, it is the problems alluded to above that make meaningful ratio analysis of the income statement and balance sheet difficult. Because the way in which financial matters are reported is management's discretion, the same line item figures for two companies, even in the same industry, may represent very different economic realities.

Thus, although HBS introduces students to ratio analysis, students are taught to focus in on cash flow analysis. HBS, as well as many financial experts, perceives this to be the one type of analysis that provides a common denominator for analyzing the financial numbers of any company. By looking at the track record, cash flow numbers can be crunched, although sometimes with great pain, to help the business analyst answer some crucial questions about the future.

Most CEOs, CFOs, and controllers are becoming increasingly less enamored of earnings per share and working capital levels as a measure of financial health. They are realizing that stock price is most directly related to the market's assessment of the strength of a company's current and anticipated cash flow. When analyzing the strengths and weaknesses of their own company's portfolio of businesses as well as their competitors', decision-makers are going beyond the traditional questions of what is the current ratio and the debt-to-worth ratio. They now ask questions about whether the business will be able to generate enough cash to finance the working capital needed to grow and replace fixed assets as they become obsolete, meet debt obligations as they come due, and pay dividends in order to survive as a healthy competitor.

CASH FLOW STATEMENT

Cash flow analysis is used to cut through the vagaries and mysteries of financial measurement and to uncover the actual sources and uses of cash in order to diagnose the health of the business and project its future.

The practice was especially popular after financial catastrophies like W.T. Grant hurt creditors. It is also interesting to note that cash flow analysis has gained even more favor as a method for analyzing a company since the introduction of portfolio analysis into many companies' strategic planning process. In portfolio analysis, managers try to determine which of their businesses are "cash cows" (able to provide cash); which are "question marks"; and which are "dogs" (in need of external funding to survive).

For HBS students without a financial background, generating a cash flow statement is one of the most grueling exercises of the course. Some students never get comfortable with the process. It challenges to the limit one's ability to understand accounting.

A number of alternative cash-flow analysis formats and techniques exist—too many to go into them in this book. We sketch here the basics and identify some key issues, and leave alternative techniques for the individual to investigate. Which format one uses will depend on the question one wants to answer. In general, however, cash flow statements reflect where cash was generated from and how it was put to use in a given period.

The sources of funds and the uses for funds are analyzed in three broad categories: operations, which is measured primarily in the income statement; investments; and financing. Investments and financing are measured primarily in the balance sheet.

Funds may be raised through operations, debt, equity; or through sale of an asset or reduction in the value of inventory. Funds may be used to service operating debt, pay dividends, buy assets, or to increase the value of inventory. These are the major sources of funds and the primary methods for utilizing them.

HBS students are taught to begin a cash flow analysis by determining the amount of cash provided or used by operations. This is done by starting with net income and then adding back to it any expenses in the income statement for which a check does not actually have to be written—such as depreciation—and by subtracting from net income any revenues or gains for which a check will not be received—such as equity in the earnings of a subsidiary overseas that is not repatriating cash.

Then, based on the balance sheet, an analysis can be done of cash sources and of cash use related to investments and financing. All else being equal, an increase in assets from one period to the next reflects a use of cash; a decrease indicates a cash source. An increase in liability or in equity reflects a source of cash and a decrease in one reflects a use of cash. This is just the beginning. Many more adjustments and refinements are necessary to produce a complete cash flow statement.

ANALYZING CASH FLOW

Once a student completes a cash flow statement, there are many ways in which to analyze it in order to answer questions about the health of the company. For instance, by comparing cash from operations to the level of debt service and dividends paid, the analyst can determine if the company actually generated enough cash internally to be able to afford the debt and dividend payments.

One of the ways first-year HBSers learn to refine their cash flow analysis is to consider the impact of inflation on the cash requirements of a business. To do this, an analysis is undertaken of the financial health of companies operating during the double-digit inflation years of the late 1970s. Students come to realize that during that period many companies could barely generate enough cash from operations to cover the rapidly rising cost of replacing depreciating equipment. There were too few, if any, real dollars left over to pay dividends.

On the surface, these companies seemed to be doing very well. But their net income was rising rapidly only because relatively low historical fixed costs were being looked at as expenses in comparison to earnings measured in inflated dollars. For companies that had a policy of paying dividends based on a payout ratio of historical net income, inflation pressures caused a cash crunch. They had to borrow in order to maintain the dividend.

Cash flow, and not the reported numbers, defines reality in most business situations. Yet some companies aim at hiding performance problems from the public eye; their managers apparently believe they can still fool people, even with so many professional analysts' eyes on their companies. A consensus developed among the students in the Control course that management's best hope for inspiring prolonged investor confidence is to signal regularly that they are aware of their financial reality and are taking the correct actions in light of that reality.

CONTROL RECOMMENDATIONS

By the end of the course, students are acutely aware of the dichotomy between the technical and subjective judgment skills required to make sound control decisions. A typical exam scenario is one in which a company has been losing profitability, and the president wants to redesign the management control systems to bring profits up.

In a comprehensive exam, HBS students would have to include the following to make a coherent recommendation.

1. A summary of the key environmental factors in the industry and business that have an impact on the control decision, including a clear statement of the company's objectives, strategy, and organizational structure.
2. A definition of the problem, and a summary of what is causing it, and of how serious and urgent a problem it is. This requires an analysis of financial statements, cash flow, the management control and information systems and of variances between the budget and actual performance. The objective is to discover whether the problem is an actual performance problem, such as poor quality products; an organizational problem, such as functional departments not working together to ser-

vice customers; a systems problem, in which the systems in place are not designed properly given the company's objectives and environment; or a combination of these problems, which is the result of change in the environment or in the organizational structure, and which requires the implementation of new control systems.

3. A summary of the reasonable options available.

4. A recommendation and rationale for action to solve problems in the short- and long-term; this rationale covers the trade-offs and risks in any action plan. The recommendation should include the objectives of the suggested changes and a description of the components of management's control methods, such as the types of responsibility centers, their objectives, as well as the variables that should be measured to track each unit's performance. In addition, a decision as to how performance should be communicated must be included.

Recommendations of this sort would be evaluated based on a student's grasp of the major issues, and on the demonstration of an artful analysis. Effective control of a business requires understanding how to design financial measurement systems that fit the context and needs of a business; and how to interpolate from financial results in order to perceive how the system as a whole serves to motivate people. The controller should know and communicate how far off course the business is from its target, and what needs to be done to bring it back on course. The controller's recommendations should play a big part in the general manager's decisions regarding marketing, finance, human resource, and production decisions, and especially those strategic decisions affecting the future direction of the business.

CONTROL CHECKLIST

These questions will help direct one's thinking about whether a company has effective management control and information systems in place.

1. Are there management controls, particularly budgeting systems, in place for each organizational unit?
2. Do managers have control over the variables in their budget for which they are responsible?
3. Are the budget objectives for each unit reasonable and are they designed to give people proper incentive to act in a manner that helps achieve the company's objectives?
4. Are the budget systems tied to the strategic planning and reward systems?
5. Are there systems in place for periodically measuring the performance of each segment of the business?
6. Do these measurement systems provide the most appropriate and meaningful information needed for managers to make sound business decisions?
7. Who's in charge of designing, implementing, and monitoring the appropriateness of the management control and information systems? Does that person have credibility and authority within the organization?
8. Does management effectively communicate its corporate performance to stakeholders?

8

MANAGERIAL ECONOMICS

There is no such thing as a Managerial Economics Department in any company we know of. But almost anyone within a corporation can benefit from adopting an ME perspective, because managerial economics is all about making decisions.

Besides encouraging students to think of each impending business decision as a tree, each of whose branches leads to a different outcome, HBS teaches that interactive business situations are much like games in which people constantly maneuver to achieve their own goals. The student who shows the most savvy is the one who makes his or her decision after fully considering how other people will react.

The three basic game scenarios that are studied in ME class are called the "zero-sum game," "prisoners' dilemma" and "battle of the sexes." Many business situations can be categorized as falling into one of these three game models. By deciding which game model a situation falls into, one may gain insight into the best course of action to take in the situation.

ZERO-SUM GAMES

In zero-sum games, if one competitor wins, the other must lose. There is a finite value of any item being competed for, and the winner takes all.

Flipping a coin is the classic example of a zero-sum game. If the coin comes up heads, it can't possibly be tails. The sum of the positive outcome—heads—and the negative outcome—tails—is zero. Hence the idea of a zero-sum game. Parimutuel horse or dog racing is another example. Those who choose the winning horse to bet on collect the money of those who bet on the horses that didn't win—the sum of all the money bet and all the money paid out (minus the percentage kept for track management; the horse owners' purse, and taxes, of course) is zero.

In business, two people may seek to be promoted to one slot, yet only one can receive the promotion. When the promotion is announced, there is one winner and one loser.

In true zero-sum situations, a player's strategic options are limited to one if winning is important. Each player must go all out. No compromises can be worked out because the winner takes all the value. Negotiation is fruitless.

PRISONERS' DILEMMA

In a prisoners' dilemma scenario, the best outcome for all involved would be achieved if each competitor does not try to maximize advantage unilaterally. Rather, all parties do better if they work together. Collective agreement on action brings the biggest payoff to the group. Individual action by each player usually leads to the worst outcome.

Let's look at the classic prisoners' dilemma matrix.

Prisoner A and Prisoner B are interrogated in separate rooms. Let us assume that conviction of someone who doesn't confess will bring a life sentence, but that the prosecution does not

PRISONER A

		CONFESS	DOESN'T CONFESS
P **R** **I** **S** **O** **N** **E** **R** **B**	CONFESS	20 YEARS	A LIFE SENTENCE B 10 YEARS
	DOESN'T CONFESS	A 10 YEARS B LIFE SENTENCE	NO CONVICTION, NO SENTENCE

FIGURE 8–1. Prisoners' Dilemma Matrix

have enough evidence without confessions to convict both men. The prosecution is willing to lessen sentences for confessions just because of the time and expense saved by not going to trial. If one man confesses and testifies, his sentence will be especially light. But if they both confess, there is no need for either to testify, and no need for the prosecution to lighten the sentence for each as much as the prosecution would have for the prisoner who confessed alone.

If prisoner A confesses and testifies against prisoner B, while prisoner B does not confess, prisoner A will get 10 years. The converse is true if prisoner B confesses and testifies against prisoner A. If both confess, saving the cost of two trials, both men will be sentenced to twenty years. If neither confesses, they will not be convicted because of lack of evidence.

As can clearly be seen, if they cooperate and hold out against confessing, they will both get the best outcome. But being locked in separate rooms and interrogated separately, their mistrust of each other can lead to both prisoners confessing— each hoping to be the one who confessed alone, and who receives the lighter sentence—leading to the worst joint outcome. Any strategy that can build the odds of both parties trusting the other and cooperating is effective in a prisoners' dilemma situation.

The airline industry experienced this type of dilemma in the mid-1980s. During the period of heavy regulation of the industry, airlines were forced to cooperate—to forswear competing on prices and routes. Now, in the deregulated environment, each airline is trying to maximize its own profits by cutting prices in order to build travel volume, and by getting in on the most lucrative routes. The result has been the worst outcome for most airlines; certainly for those that were established before deregulation and that have long-standing labor contracts, and few ways to cut costs. If competing carriers all kept their fares up all would probably benefit. Luckily, for consumers, antitrust laws prohibit such explicit price-fixing.

If the airlines find that the market for travel becomes finite, the game will shift from a prisoners' dilemma situation more toward a zero-sum game.

BATTLE OF THE SEXES

The battle of the sexes is a dilemma common in marriage or any other close relationship. The best outcome for one player is achieved when the other player stops pursuing his or her best options so the first player can achieve his or her goals.

Each of a number of companies, let us say, can make a product to satisfy a particular market need. But really only one such product can be economically viable in the market, because the fixed costs of production are so high that each company needs the revenues from a large share of the market in order to make any return on its investment.

In this type of scenario, communication and signals between

the interested parties is crucial so that competitors do not enter the market: It's not advantageous for any party to have the probable losers compete. Announcements about future product introductions are often made to keep competitors from even considering entering the marketplace. Being there first is important in determining who will have to give in.

ME provides a quantitative framework for decision-making in situations where many people believe gut feelings do just fine. Much of the class was shown how misleading gut feeling can be when we studied a case on car insurance. Our ME analysis demonstrated how insurance companies make excessive profits on average drivers who buy low-deductible collision insurance. A show of hands demonstrated that the divine wisdom of 90 percent of the HBS student body, as practiced by each student in real life, was to purchase the low deductible— to pay excessively high rates and help fund the insurance companies' profit-sharing plan. Once a careful analysis was complete, 100 percent of the HBS class saw that the extra cost was not justified.

Our objectives for this chapter are to make explicit the fundamental quantitative decision-making framework HBS espouses. Although the details of all the analysis are beyond the chapter's scope, the framework developed here will enable one to break down complex decisions into their most simple components. This notion is introduced in the first three months of the first year at HBS and is used through the remaining two years as a basis for thinking through decisions presented in the various functional disciplines.

ME is a Quantitative Analysis Jock's delight, since at some point in the analysis there is the chance of backing into a "right" answer. But it is equally exciting for students good at making decisions based on subjective judgments and common sense to learn how to quantify and make explicit all aspects of a decision. One of the ironic things HBS students come to realize in this course is that in order to accurately quantify a decision using ME techniques, it helps to have an intuitive understanding of the components of the decision.

Good judgment remains the key to making good decisions. But the ME course helps provide more complete information about the alternatives being faced; it provides a framework and tools for analyzing the value of each option available. The quantitative techniques students learn are helpful for evaluating the potential value of alternative strategies, forecasting future uncertainties, taking into account attitudes toward risk, anticipating competitive reactions using game theory, and for allocating resources through linear programming.

Not only does the language of ME give the analyst a methodology for thinking through the options at hand, it also allows the analyst to share that thought process explicitly with other people. A decision based on gut feeling alone cannot be communicated with the same degree of clarity. Another major advantage of the decision-tree approach is that if others have information relevant to the decision that the analyst has not considered, the data can easily be incorporated into the analysis. And, if others have predictions about the future that differ from the analyst's, the different predictions can be tested in the decision-tree model to see if they would indicate a different course of action. Thus, the decision-tree model facilitates the communications of ideas and the flow of information, two factors whose absence often hinders the best decisions from emerging.

Another facet to ME analysis is that it is conducive to *sensitivity analysis.* Sensitivity analysis tests how dependent the ultimate decision is on the assumptions and forecasts of the future. One can test best- and worst-case scenarios. Sensitivity analysis also allows one to test other people's assumptions, should they differ.

The range of decisions studied in the ME course is wide. A few examples follow:

- The head of marketing for a major-league baseball franchise trying to determine which variables had the greatest impact on home-game attendance over the past several years, and what those variables indicate about future marketing efforts.

- The head of operations at a major winery faced with an inpending storm that, depending on its longevity and intensity, has the potential either to destroy the crop or to make it one of the best in the company's history. Do we harvest now, or take our chances?
- A division president trying to decide whether to make a bid on oil-drilling rights in an attractive but as yet unproven field, and if so at what price.

THE DECISION TREE— MAPPING THE ALTERNATIVES

The underpinning of all ME analysis taught at HBS is the *decision tree*. It depicts the alternative strategies available to the decision-maker.

A decision tree is made up of points where the decision-maker must make a decision (represented by a box), other points where an event will happen that the decision-maker has no control over (represented by a circle), and branches emanating from each of these points.

The branches represent the alternative actions and alternative events that could occur at each step along the way. The tree begins with a decision box. At the end of every branch, the decision-maker must ask, What then? Does a decision have to be made or will an event occur? This questioning process drives the drawing of the tree.

Let's walk through a simple example to illustrate the fundamentals of building a decision tree.

BUILDING A DECISION TREE

The product manager of a new sugarless mint is faced with the decision whether to launch the product or simply scrap the project. This decision called for would be represented in ME language by figure 8–2, which begins the decision tree.

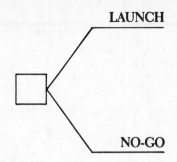

FIGURE 8-2. Decision Tree Step One

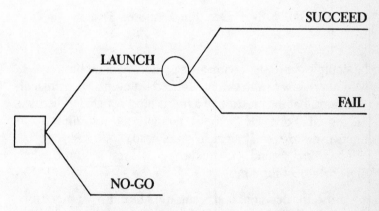

FIGURE 8-3. Decision Tree Step Two

If the product is launched, then one of two things will happen. Either it will be successful or it will fail. These possible outcomes of an uncertain event would be represented by the **"event node"** and branches on the tree in figure 8-3.

If the product is scrapped, then the product manager perceives that to be the end point of the scrap strategy. This judgment would be represented on the tree by the bold-faced branch in figure 8-4.

The example here is simple and straightforward. However, many of the trees that the decision-maker maps out will likely

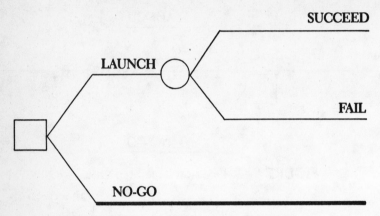

FIGURE 8–4. Decision Tree Step Three

be complex monsters with at least twenty branches, replete with alternatives strategies and uncertain events. It is in such situations that the creation of a tree is most beneficial, because the format allows one to lay out thoughts too voluminous and interwoven to keep straight in one's head.

There are several basic concepts to keep in mind when drawing a decision tree.

- First, the decisions and events must be drawn in the chronological sequence in which they happen.
- Second, the alternative actions or possible events included in the tree must be mutually exclusive, and the investigation of alternatives must be exhaustive.
- Third, the decision-maker must decide the time horizon over which to evaluate the consequences of the first decision. Decision trees could conceivably grow forever if an end point were not decided on.

    When trying to decide which actions to take, one must remember that for every action taken, competitors may have a reaction. ME trains students to anticipate what each of these reactions may be and to plan actions accordingly. Students assess how well off each competitor would be under each scenario. Then they chose a strategy that seems the most advantageous for a particular company.

- Fourth, a decision tree allows one to plan a strategy for action depending upon how certain events work out. It is important to note that a decision tree reflects the decision-maker's perception of the opportunities for action at each decision point.

ASSESSING END POINT VALUES

After laying out the alternatives for action and the possible outcomes, the decision-maker needs to assign a cash value to each of the possible outcomes. HBS students do this by analyzing the present value of the cash flows to be derived from each strategy. Thus, they must capture all the relevant revenues that would be produced and the costs that would be incurred by following each of the decision tree's branches. Not included in the analysis of revenues and costs are sunk costs—money spent regardless of the decision; allocated costs over which one has no control; and noncash expenses, such as depreciation, and financing costs which should be considered separately from an investment decision.

HBSers get it drummed into their heads that they must be sure to calculate all cash flows on either a before-tax or after-tax basis (usually the latter) for comparability. Second, each outcome value must take the time value of money into account. Each should be expressed in present value terms. The discount factor used should be consistent with before-tax or after-tax cash flow. It can be either the weighted average cost of capital (chapter 4) or the reinvestment rate—the rate at which an extra dollar could be invested by the decision-maker.

On the next page is an example of what the projected cash flow from the product launch alternatives may look like.

In the new-product launch decision, the product manager determined that the present value of the relevant after-tax cash flows anticipated from a successful product launch would be

$5.5 million; and that the company would likely lose $3.5 million in a failed launch attempt. Scrapping the product at this point would cost nothing beyond the costs already sunk in development. An HBS student would depict these end-point assessments as shown in figure 8–5.

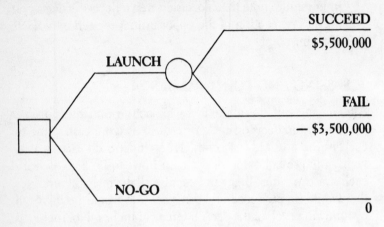

FIGURE 8–5. End-point Assessments

It is obvious that tremendous amounts of judgment go into determining end-point values. Assumptions and steps taken in determining them should be recorded.

ASSESSING PROBABILITIES

After laying out all of the alternatives for outcomes, the next challenge is to predict the possibility of each alternative occurring.

When flipping a coin, the probability of a head or tail occurring is each .5. The probability of any of the six faces of a die showing is one out of six, or .16.

The product manager can make a prediction, based on his experience with prior product launches, that the probability for success would be .3, or 30 percent, and that the probability for failure would be .7, or 70 percent. These predictions are expressed in ME language in figure 8–6.

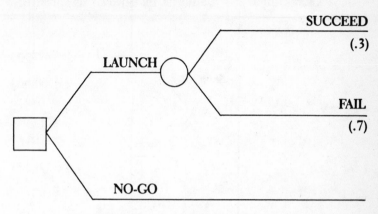

FIGURE 8–6. Probability Assessment

Note that in every case, the sum of the alternative probabilities at each event node must add up to 1.0, or 100 percent.

Again, judgment plays a big role. The probability assigned to a particular outcome is a guess, a prediction, or a forecast. In some cases the decision-maker will have prior knowledge or historical data that helps in making a more educated prediction about the probability of outcomes.

EXPECTED MONETARY VALUE ANALYSIS— SOLVING THE TREE

What does all this work do toward getting one closer to a decision?

First, assume that one wants to take the course of action that is likely, on average, to yield the highest monetary value based on all of the input about outcomes and probabilities. If so, once the tree is filled out, the next step is to "solve" the decision tree by "folding back" and "pruning" branches to determine which action strategy is likely to have the biggest payoff. To do this, HBSers learn to start at the end-point values. Then they calculate the expected monetary value (EMV) of an event node as the weighted average of the outcome values.

Our product launch tree would be folded back as shown in figure 8–7.

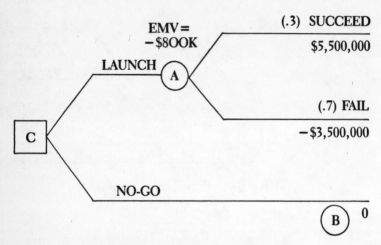

FIGURE 8–7. Folding Back the Tree

The EMV at point A would be calculated as follows: ($5,500,000 × .3)+(–$3,500,000 × .7) = –$800,000. On average, then, the company would expect to lose $800,000 if it launched the product based on EMV. Intuitively, this does not look like a wise investment. And, the ME techniques prove the intuition correct.

At a decision box, such as point C, the decision-maker would choose the alternative with the highest estimated value and prune back or reject the other alternatives. In this case, the "no-go" value of zero at point B looks more attractive than the negative EMV at point A. So, the launch branch is pruned, "no go" is chosen and the EMV of the product launch decision is zero.

The tree in figure 8–8 depicts the above in ME language, which is how students would represent the problem in an exam.

All the analysis done so far indicates the product manager should forget the idea of launching the product. But what if

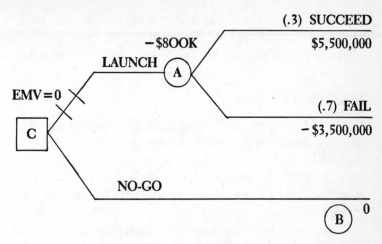

FIGURE 8–8. Choosing No-Go

it were possible to collect more information about the market's perception of the product?

FORECASTING

There are many ways to gain more information to help forecast more accurately. And there are two major forecasting tricks. One is to be sure that the information one is gathering will actually help one forecast more accurately. The second is not to spend more money and time collecting the data than it's worth. Many marketing people wish they had considered that question after they get back confusing, unreasonable test-market or copy-test results.

There are several techniques for forecasting the outcome of future events based on historical data.

ABSOLUTE-ERROR FORECASTING

The absolute-error model, a forecasting technique, is very simple. It's effective when one is aware that a forecaster is consistently wrong by the same amount.

If the marketing department is usually 10 percent too aggressive with its sales forecasts, the ME decision-maker may choose to reduce the marketing department's forecasts by 10 percent. It is obvious how important it is to know the track record of people who are helping to forecast future outcomes.

REGRESSION ANALYSIS

Regression analysis, much more complex than forecasting, is accomplished with the help of a computer. The concept is an eyebrow raiser. One can always tell that an MBA or Ph.D. economist is in the room when regression analysis is constantly mentioned; the phrase sets off warning bells in many people's minds.

A regression analysis is a computer modeling technique that forecasts future results by requiring its user to identify all the major factors that influenced events in past situations similar to the ones currently being analyzed.

Let's look at an HBS case requiring students to predict attendance at a major league baseball team's home games next season—a case that lends itself well to regression analysis.

Consider all of the possible factors that influence game attendance—the opposing team, game time, time of the season, day of the week, average ticket price, star players on both the visiting team and the home team, temperature, television coverage, and the number of games by which each team is out of first place. Feed information about each of these variables, plus attendance figures for each game, into the computer for several past seasons.

Using a regression analysis program, the computer can then go through thousands of integrations, generating information about which variables historically have had the most influence on attendance. Straight regression analysis assumes that the historical relationships between influential factors and the outcomes will remain the same in the future.

Interpretation of our results when we did this problem in the fall of 1981 told us that the strongest influences on attendance were the presence of star players, and teams' nearness to first place. An interesting and valuable finding for management was that local television coverage of the game did not hurt attendance.

Those results may help to explain why the New York Knicks were willing to pay so much for Patrick Ewing or why Doug Flutie's salary was so high in 1985. Of course, this all looks like a firm grasp of the obvious. But it's nice to know that occasionally analysis bears out intuition.

SAMPLING

Another way that a decision-maker can collect additional forecast data is to take a representative sample of outcomes and predict an outcome based on the results of the sampling. Marketers are big believers in this technique, and call it *test marketing*.

The product manager of the new sugarless mint may try to market the product in one or two representative towns in an area in which he believes the response to the product will reliably predict the response to a nationwide introduction of the product. The larger the sample, the more accurate the information collected may be. The trade-off is that test marketing and sampling cost lots of money and time up front and yield no guarantees, only more information.

The question managers must always ask is: How much money should we spend to get better information?

The ME course teaches students how to refine that question. The theory is that a decision-maker should never pay more than the value of perfect information for less-than-perfect information. So, the maximum amount that should be paid for information is the value of perfect information—the gain that a decision-maker would realize if the information leads to the *perfect* decision. An illustration of how this might work can be seen in the contemplated launch of the new mint. The product manager forecasted, without test marketing, that there was a 30 percent chance of a successful launch and a 70 percent chance of failure. He would choose the strategy with the highest EMV, which in this case is the "no-go" alternative. (See figure 8–8.)

If, on the other hand, the product manager could test market and get perfect information that told him that there would definitely be a 30 percent chance of success and a 70 percent chance of failure, and if he acted on this information so that when the perfect information predicted failure, he would choose not to launch, then this scenario would be depicted as shown in figure 8–9.

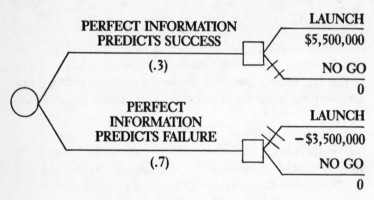

FIGURE 8–9. Perfect Information

The EMV suggested by this scenario, in which the launch decision is based on perfect information, would be $1,650,000, as shown in figure 8–10.

In this case the value of perfect information would be $1,650,000—the difference between the expected average payoff on the original decision of no investment, and that on the "perfect" decision.

If the product manager does not believe he could run a meaningful market test for less than $1.65 million, he should not bother to test market at all and should make the decision based on the best information he has at the moment.

It should be apparent intuitively that the less predictive power the sampling technique has, the less should be paid for it.

SENSITIVITY ANALYSIS

What if the product manager did not think a test market would

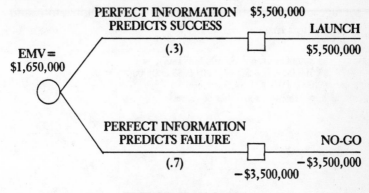

FIGURE EMV 8–10.

be advantageous, but still wasn't sure that the assumptions built into his initial tree were correct and did not want to give up on the product yet?

HBS students learn several types of sensitivity analysis to test how important their assumptions are to a particular decision. The types that we will discuss briefly are *break-even analysis* and *nonmonetary value assessment*. The major point here is that once the basic decision tree is drawn, the analyst's job is not over. All key input into the equation must be reevaluated to test the limitations of the decisions being made.

The product manager may wonder whether his guesstimates of the probability of success and failure are accurate. To test the sensitivity of his assumptions, the product manager can ask, How likely would a successful launch have to be in order for the product launch to be at least as attractive an option as scrapping the project? A break-even analysis is an effective way to answer this type of question.

In the language of ME, this problem translates as follows: At what probability of success does the EMV of the launch strategy (point A in figure 8–11) equal that of the "no-go" strategy?

If the primary variable—the probability of success—is X, then by definition the probability of failure is 1–X. The EMV of the launch strategy is calculated based on the weighted average of the possible outcomes of $5.5 million profit and $3.5 million loss.

$$\$5,500,000(X) + [-\$3,500,000(1-X)] = 0$$
$$\$5,500,000(X) - \$3,500,000 + \$3,500,000(X) = 0$$
$$\$9,000,000(X) = \$3,500,000$$
$$X = .389 = \text{probability of success}$$

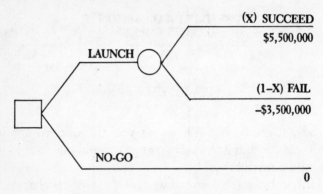

FIGURE 8–11. Probability of Success

Thus, if the probability of success exceeds .389 or 38.9 percent, the launch would be more attractive than the "no-go" option if the decision is made on the basis of maximizing EMV. It is sometimes easier for a decision-maker to assess the likelihood of an outcome from this angle. If the product manager doubts that there is a 39 percent chance of success, then he will probably still scrap the launch. However, he may go ahead with it if he thinks the odds for success are about 40 percent.

Another factor the product manager could consider in his analysis is the nonmonetary factors that are important to his decision, such as the potential clout with the retailers that the company would enjoy if it could add a sugarless mint to its product line. HBS students ask how much this clout needs to be worth to reverse the decision to scrap the launch.

This is done by adding a variable ("C") to the end-point value of the successful launch possibility—C represents that unknown but positive factor—clout. Then students do a break-even analysis and solve for C.

The calculation to solve for the value of C is based on the same principle discussed above. The relevant decision-tree and algebraic calculations are shown in figure 8–12.

$$[(5,500,000 + C) \times .3] + (-\$3,500,000 \times .7) = 0$$
$$1,650,000 + .3C - 2,450,000 = 0$$
$$C = \$2,666,667$$

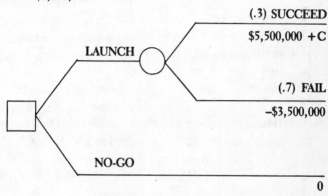

FIGURE 8–12. C Factor

That bit of homework tells students that the clout would have to be worth more than $2.7 million for the company to go ahead with the product launch, assuming a 30 percent chance that the launch would succeed. That's a lot of clout. If the product manager does not think that an investment exceeding $2.7 million in clout is worth it, the decision not to launch should stand.

What if the product manager is still not satisfied with his analysis of the decision? What if he wants to know which decision he would make on criteria other than EMV?

HBS students would ask how much risk he will incur, or how averse he is to risk. If he wanted the challenge and opportunity for upside payoff, then he should launch the product and see what happens. Maybe he will get lucky and get the $5.5-million brass ring. If he were on a very tight budget and could not afford to lose $3.5 million, then given his basic assumptions, he should forget the launch.

HBS teaches future managers that the risk profile or level of tolerance for risk that each person or business has is extremely important in making decisions. Because decisions are not always made on the basis of maximizing EMV, it's crucial to agree upon the decision criteria before starting the analysis.

COMPUTERIZED DECISION TREES

Two techniques are introduced at HBS for solving problems having so many options that it is virtually impossible to solve the problems in your head, or even with a scratch pad. Computers are used for these two techniques.

The first technique involves using a *simulation model.* A typical decision may involve calculating the number of hula hoops that should be produced in the current year. Hula hoops are a fad product; the possibilities of the level of demand and production that could be assumed are so numerous that this decision tree would have infinite numbers of branches. This problem is best solved by computer.

Running a simulation model is akin to taking a representative sample of the possible values that the uncertain quantities could take on. The model simulates what may actually happen in the world to affect the outcome of each strategy, and it enables one to run through many iterations of the decision tree, assigning new values to uncertainties each time through based on a random walk. It generates an EMV for each strategy based on the average of the payoffs from each trial.

The computer also makes it easy to test assumptions, and to conduct sensitivity analyses.

The second technique, *linear programming,* is used primarily to help decide how to allocate resources most productively. An objective is set, usually to maximize profits or minimize costs. Constraints are listed, such as hourly production capacity on each machine and by each worker, hours of operation, raw material content of each product, or warehouse capacity. The computer then solves the many resulting simultaneous equations students provide. By interpreting the output, students know how many of each product should be made to maximize profits, which areas of production will be at or under capacity at the optimal solution level; whether it would be profitable to introduce a new product. And they have answers to a host of other questions as well. Linear programming is often used to help solve problems about maximizing return in an investment portfolio.

Most of the more in-depth techniques for helping quantify decision-making judgments are built on either simulation models or on linear programming models.

ME-BASED RECOMMENDATIONS

Once the situation has been analyzed to death, how does one make a decision?

There are two major elements to keep in mind when choosing a strategy for action.

First, a decision tree represents only a particular decision-maker's perspective, because the opportunities for action vary and each person's assessment of the outcome of each uncertain event differs.

Second, as new information is gained or the situation changes, the tree may have to be changed; any single decision tree represents only a static picture of a situation.

When choosing a strategy of action, it may be helpful to use the following steps:

Step One:
Decide explicitly on the criteria for making the decision. Is the objective to maximize EMV? Minimize the risk of losing money? Minimize the risk of damaging one's reputation? Choose the decision criteria that best fit with one's strategy and values.

Step Two:
Decide explicitly on the time frame to be considered in making this decision. Is the purpose to consider the potential

long-term risks and returns, or to focus only on the immediate possible outcomes? Is it necessary to look six months into the future? A year? Two years? Farther?

Step Three:
Although one should work hard to include in a decision tree all the key issues that may arise, be sure to rethink the potential problems and values of each strategy. Consider all of the possible competitive reactions to and consequences of any action. Are there any critical forks in the tree that indicate it would be worth trying to gather more information about the probability of particular outcomes? If one used sampling techniques to predict the likelihood of outcomes, are the results reliable enough to stake a decision on them?

Most business decisions are complex, with many factors to weigh and consider. Good judgment is the key to making good decisions. By making the many factors explicit, showing their interrelationships, and breaking the big question down into component factors, quantitative analysis can sometimes lead to better decisions. Sometimes it can be more trouble than it's worth; and if not done correctly, it can be downright misleading. Judgment and instinct are essential to making proper management decisions, including decisions derived quantitatively.

MANAGEMENT ECONOMICS CHECKLIST

To assess quickly whether ME techniques are being correctly utilized, consider the following:

1. Has the decision that needs to be made been clearly stated?
2. Have the criteria for making the decision been clearly stated and agreed upon?
3. Has the decision tree been drawn correctly? Does it take into account all relevant decision points and event nodes?
4. Have end-point values been accurately calculated?

5. Have all nonmonetary values been carefully assessed?
6. Have all probabilities been accurately forecast?
7. When the tree is folded back, does the EMV-based decision make intuitive sense?

9

MANAGEMENT COMMUNICATION

The topic: Mobil Oil Company's reasons for spending millions of dollars throughout the late 1970s and early 1980s to run what have come to be known as "advertorials" in prestigious American newspapers and magazines.

The assignment: Prepare a ten-minute speech on the topic and deliver it to a Harvard Business School section of eighty-five students, one instructor, and one videotape camera, as part of the Management Communication class.

The stakes: 25 percent of the course grade and a lot of HBS pride.

It should have been a great speech.

At least six or seven hours of work went into preparation. The Mobil Oil case had been read, analyzed, reread, and reanalyzed. A careful consideration of the audiences had been made. An outline was drawn up. Note cards were prepared and several practice runs in front of the bathroom mirror had gone reasonably well. The speech outline was intelligent. In practice the speech took about eleven minutes—certainly it could be tightened to ten minutes in the highly charged atmosphere of the real presentation. After all, this student had performed excellently in class discussions all year and had significant presentation experience prior to attending HBS.

Finally, the camera rolled and the ten-minute timer began, as did the lesson in humility.

Sixty seconds somehow disappeared in the process of walking to the center of the room and saying good afternoon to the audience in a relaxed manner. It had not been necessary to introduce oneself to the bathroom mirror.

On the way down the classroom stairs to center stage, an edge of the Bermuda Triangle must have been crossed. The speaker's note cards, perfectly ordered a moment ago, somehow had got into disarray. A nonchalant glance at the top card's note to "Thank audience for listening so attentively for last ten minutes and announce that time is up" sparked instant panic.

The opening joke bombed badly, even though Carson had made it look so easy and sound so funny the night before.

Having to turn constantly to address the left, center, and right sections of the room didn't help either. It takes precious seconds to look to the left, look to the right, look center, and gaze at the camera in order to create eye contact all over the amphitheater-shaped room.

In the bathroom practice sessions, no one in the third row fell asleep. Nor did anyone come in late, slamming the door. Worst of all, the points that had emerged so easily, veritable pearls strung on a wire of smooth transitions, were now, before a live audience, produced only laboriously.

When the instructor waved her white card, signaling that only one of the allotted ten minutes remained, the speaker's heart hit his wing tips (all speeches were given in business attire), as barely half of the planned outline had been covered.

Only an abbreviated ending delivered at breakneck speed— à la Federal Express's advertisement about sending Peter to Pittsburgh—saved the speaker from the sheep hook used on students who ran past the eleven-minute mark.

It had not been a good day at HBS.

Sitting and watching the videotape while doing a critique with the professor wasn't any better. The first half of the speech was paced so slowly it resembled a Senate filibuster. The second half had an unsettling resemblance to one of those UHF television station ads with an announcer trying to sell a Vegamatic, twelve steak knives, a miracle knife sharpener that doubles as a juicer, and the world's sharpest inch-long shish kebab spears, all in sixty seconds.

It wasn't easy to watch the speaker pivot left and right enough times to wear a hole in the carpet, yet somehow manage to have his back to most of the people most of the time. He had sweat on his brow by the end, threw in a few "y'know"s for good measure, and was smiling about as much as Richard Nixon in his famous "I am not a crook" speech.

THE NEED FOR STRONG COMMUNICATIONS SKILLS

Through the decades, students in HBS classes have endured experiences similar to that one, making them realize how important strong communication skills are to succeeding in the real business world. The Management Communication course, or a writing assignment, or the final exam points out to them that one can analyze until blue in the face and have the most brilliant ideas in the world, but if one can't communicate the ideas clearly and persuasively to the right people, intelligence is of limited value and managerial effectiveness will be sharply diminished.

That's a particularly important but difficult lesson for many HBS students, who leave school believing new colleagues will be dying to hear their analyses and ideas just because they have such fine training.

Many MBAs find that just the opposite is true. More experienced people often are resentful of hearing from the new kid on the block, or are reflexively prone to criticize the report submitted by "that HBS asshole." MBAs actually need much-better-than-average communication skills to get their thoughts adequately considered by their peers and bosses. Yet too many find they don't have those skills.

In every poll of senior management who have hired MBAs, one of the strongest criticisms of graduate business education is the schools' failure to develop strong oral and written skills in their students.

HBS'S COMMITMENT TO COMMUNICATIONS SKILLS BUILDING

HBS stresses strong communication day in and day out through classroom case discussion, study group sessions, and the ever popular four-hour written exams. But the curriculum takes an additional step by making Management Communication (MC) a required first-year course. MC drills students in the basics of strong communications; it also involves specific exercises in many business communications areas, including:

- Internal memoranda
- Full written reports
- Group reports
- Hiring notices
- Termination notices
- Press releases
- Annual reports
- Letters seeking employment
- Prepared speeches
- Spontaneous dealings with the media
- Interviewing techniques
- Meeting discussion techniques.

While many students begin the HBS Management Communications course thinking it will be a soft course, Harvard's serious treatment of the subject matter quickly becomes evident.

As the course progresses, many HBSers realize they have a lot to learn from the course—especially from the required writing and speaking assignments—and they take it very seriously. Even so, many students experience disasters like the one related earlier at least once or twice during the course; but with luck (aided by effort), they may one day look back upon those experiences as lessons learned indelibly, in the lab.

THE ROLE OF THE MC DECISION-MAKER

Management communication plays an important part at every level of one's management career. There is almost no business or position that does not require effective communication with other people to get the job done.

MC cases cover a wide range of decision-maker positions, including the following:

- An officer in charge of hiring, who must screen applications to choose candidates to be interviewed, and who later must write letters to communicate the company's decision on hiring to all candidates
- A public relations officer issuing a press release to local media representatives regarding a company's proposed environmental protection actions
- A CEO whose most profitable product is being recalled from stores nationwide, trying to decide how to manage crisis communications
- A business-unit manager deciding how to communicate pending layoffs both to those being let go and to those being retained.

Management Communication is one of the most tangible courses in the first-year HBS curriculum. Not only are students asked to analyze business situations and develop recommendations; they must go an extra step to develop the exact written or oral communication they believe best addresses the situation at hand. Memos, reports, graphic presentations, speeches and press releases all get developed on tight timetables over the course of the year. Assignments are expected to be free of errors, perfectly typed, and handed in on time under penalty of almost certain rejection if these criteria are not met.

Students' speeches and writings are always critiqued by peers as well as by instructors. This intensifies the pressure to do good work. Peer opinion is a strong motivator. Most MBA graduates find that their written and oral communications are closely scrutinized by coworkers when they begin work. We have all heard tales of the company grammarian who will send back memos corrected. What to say, how to say it, and whom to say it to are all decisions that must be considered carefully, because human communication so often lends itself to misinterpretation.

THE IMPORTANCE OF EFFECTIVE MANAGEMENT COMMUNICATION

Effective management communication has always been important in business, but as we move into a world that is increasingly media-intensive, effective communication skills are becoming even more important. As the job market becomes more competitive, managers who can present ideas clearly and persuasively stand the best chance of being effective, and of progressing in their company and in their field. As managers near the top of their organization, proven strengths in dealing with both internal and external group communications may well become a prerequisite for advancement.

It is easy to see in recent events examples of the importance of effective management communication.

One extreme example is that of the first Tylenol poisoning scare, in 1981. With the discovery of several bottles of Tylenol that had been poisoned, one of the most successful and profitable product lines in American business was threatened with extinction. Within seventy-two hours, as the media spread the story across the country, Johnson & Johnson, Tylenol's maker, was faced with the task of developing a communication program to restore the entire nation's confidence in a product that suddenly was linked with several deaths. Another task was developing a safer product. Consumers were justifiably afraid of using Tylenol, and they had many alternative brands to turn to.

Any mistakes in the management communication strategy or in its execution could have cost J&J hundreds of millions of dollars. Analysts had already begun slashing J&J's earnings estimates and predicting extinction of the brand.

J&J top management got involved in the crisis within hours of the first news of the problem. A task force of experts in all aspects of communication—advertising, public relations, financial community relations, public-opinion polling, and government relations—as well as J&J managers, was assembled immediately. They monitored the situation on a daily basis. Situations were thought through carefully and all options assessed. Decisions were made immediately, as was necessary.

Most important, however, was that J&J managers made the right decisions. There was never any hint of a cover-up or of profits being given priority over consumer safety. J&J rejected government advice and voluntarily removed every bottle of Tylenol in America from store shelves, tested them, and destroyed them. Consumers and retailers were educated about the problem and invited to return Tylenol for refunds. All government efforts were cooperated with fully. Wall Street and all J&J employees were kept informed. All actions were done at J&J's expense, as company managers decided to invest millions of dollars in the short term in an effort to act responsibly and gain long-term benefit.

Tylenol was held off the market until consumers' fears calmed down. It was returned in new, tamper-resistant packaging, and was supported by a specially designed advertising and public relations campaign.

It turned out tragically that the tamper-*resistant* packaging was just that, and not tamper-*proof*. The second Tylenol poisoning scare, in 1986, proved that J&J had not solved the packaging problem. To their credit, though, J&J's top management had already decided to introduce a new product form, the Caplet, and they moved quickly to control the damage from the second scare.

Brilliant management communication strategy and execution efforts saved the Tylenol brand in 1981, and saved Johnson & Johnson, its employees, and its stockholders literally hundreds of millions of dollars over the long haul. The fate of the Tylenol Caplet remains to be seen.

Contrast J&J's managers' handling of the Tylenol crisis with the manner in which communication is handled in other companies.

How often does one see examples of poor communication in the typical corporation: Someone is promoted, but the announcement is made improperly. Someone is fired and rumors abound, but no communication is issued to clear the air. An acquisition is made, but employees are the last to know. One's in-box receives fifteen memos a day, only two of which are worth reading. The boss is issuing orders and everyone jumps, but no one is quite sure of the reasoning behind the directions.

How often does someone call on the phone, walk into an office, or interrupt a meeting to say something that almost seems calculated to create conflict? MBAs are famous for doing that.

Glance at almost any newspaper or magazine headline relating to business and the importance of management communication is evident.

Lee Iacocca's strengths in this area have been an almost invaluable asset to Chrysler throughout its rebuilding process. In contrast, the lack of communication skills shown by the leadership of Bank of Boston hurt the company greatly in dealing with the news that the bank had been fined for illegal international cash transactions made in the early 1980s. In 1986 the jury is still out on how well E.F. Hutton's managers will manage communication to the public, the press, its own employees, and federal investigators as further inquiries are made into its previously reported check-kiting activities.

Management communication issues clearly come in all shapes and sizes. Some, such as J&J's management of the

Tylenol crisis or Union Carbide's handling of the poison-gas disaster in Bhopal, India, are massive in scope and clearly result in huge monetary savings or losses; others, such as writing a clear memo to subordinates or saying things tactfully to a fellow employee almost go unnoticed and have little immediate impact.

In the MC course at HBS, students discuss all these types of situations and are made aware of how frequently everyone at all levels in business management must make communication decisions—and of how important making the right decisions is in the quest to become an effective general manager.

LOOK BEFORE YOU LEAP

One of the points made first and repeated most often in the Management Communication class at HBS is that, consciously or otherwise, the typical manager makes many significant communication decisions each day—all the way from saying hello to the boss in the morning, to deciding who to include on the copy list for important memos, to deciding when to leave the office each evening—and that care must be taken to think about these decisions in order to make the right ones. Too often, we make major communications decisions without thinking them through at all. Or we just say or write whatever first comes to mind.

From working through a series of MC cases, students come to realize that managers are constantly sending signals to everyone they work with, and those signals must be sent with care.

In one case, a manager worked hard to craft the best possible way to let some employees know that they were going to be laid off due to slumping sales, only to realize, once the news was out, that he had totally forgot to carefully communicate reassuring signals to the 95 percent of his employees who were not being let go but were wondering if they would be next.

The case studies also reveal that managers usually have many communications options open to them in any given situation. For example, a product manager learns that a competitor is planning to introduce a new product in market test. She has to decide who to tell about this, whether to do it by phone or memo or report, how quickly to communicate the information, and what exactly to say.

There are always choices to be made. The most effective managers will make them quickly, but also wisely.

The business world, like an HBS class discussion, moves very fast. People are busy, hassled, distracted. To have any chance of getting an idea, request, or question heard and remembered, one must be very clear about what one wants to say, and one must say it concisely.

Fran has a client who never stops teaching that lesson. He is director of marketing for a leading distributor of imported beers in the United States and is very busy. He often has someone in his office when Fran reaches him by phone, which Fran tries to do once a day. If Fran hasn't got his message across by the third sentence, he starts talking to his visitor. Fran's choices are then to shut up and try again in a minute or two, or spit that point out immediately in hopes of drawing him back to the conversation.

The client's strategy isn't altogether without merit. Fran usually can get to the point in a sentence or two, and it saves them both a lot of time.

HBS class discussions actually prepare students quite well for such real-world situations. HBSers learn fast that they must get their point across clearly and quickly if it is to be heeded by fellow students and the instructor. Making one strong point is usually much more memorable than chipping in a number of weaker efforts.

A scene reenacted year after year at HBS is that of eighty-four people rolling their eyes heavenward, doodling, launching spitballs, and daydreaming as a long-winded classmate gorges on air time. Chances are that student will not be called on again by that instructor for many classes to come. The students who win the most respect and get the best grades for classroom participation at HBS are those who quickly and clearly contribute one point that moves the discussion ahead.

SELECT THE MESSAGE CLEARLY

One technique many HBSers find useful in class and on the job after graduation is to jot down an outline of one, two, or maybe three topics that absolutely must be covered in an upcoming phone call or meeting, and to mentally rehearse before beginning to speak. That can help even the best communicator to be more clear and more concise. Mark McCormack, author of the best-selling book *What They Don't Teach You at the Harvard Business School*, tells the story of one of the best senior executives he knows who will often spend ten minutes preparing for a thirty-second phone call.

Given the goal of knowing exactly what to say, HBS students pursue a four-step process to select the best possible message for any given situation.

Step One
Consider the situation and determine what all the possible communication options are. Should one go into great detail or little? How much background should be given? Should one make a recommendation or not? How strongly should one come across? Should one speak now or wait a day or a week, or maybe not respond at all? To whom should the message be directed? Are there others one should communicate with?

Many experienced managers find that they naturally, almost unconsciously, do such option-screening. Less-experienced managers need to work their way through it consciously, maybe even with a scratch pad and pen. To select the best option, it often helps to lay all possibilities out on the table for review.

Step Two
Stand back from the options developed and ask, What is it that really *must* be said?

Step Three
The third step comes quickly on top of the second. Ask,

What should be said, given the politics and the personalities involved? In some MC cases, it seemed clear that saying less was better. Other times, the situation being examined demanded that questions be answered to ensure that all parties could move on to the appropriate next steps.

Step Four
Determine exactly how to convey the message determined to be correct based on steps one through three. Should it be done in a phone call, a letter, or in a face-to-face meeting? Which exact words and tone of voice should be used?

Every student's work in MC is thoroughly evaluated by the class instructor and by one or more fellow students. The advice stressed over and over again includes the following recommendations:

- Use words carefully; say exactly what is intended.
- Be concise.
- Tailor language and style to fit the audience.
- Be very clear about the actions one wishes others to take.
- If assertions are made, include clear support for them.
- Anticipate questions and answer them (before they're asked) in the initial communication. This saves time and increases persuasiveness.

The last point is particularly important. More often than not, one can't order people to do things in the business world. One must persuade them to act according to one's wishes. The more effectively communication—whether written, or spoken over the phone or in person—is able to answer all conceivable questions, the more likely the person or persons being addressed will be able to respond favorably.

Take the case of a memo to a subordinate asking for some action. How often does it occur that a subordinate has to be called up a week later with a second request for a previously requested item, and then responds, "Oh, yes, I haven't done anything yet because I had a couple of questions about that."

HBS stresses the need to anticipate and answer questions up front, in order to expedite action.

ANALYZE THE AUDIENCE THOROUGHLY

Anticipating the audience's questions is only one aspect of audience analysis stressed in MC.

Some additional issues that must be considered include the following:

- Who makes up the audience?
- How much do they know about the topic?
- How much do they want to know?
- How receptive will they be to the message?
- Of the things that could be said, which are most likely to hit home with this particular audience?

In addition to knowing the primary audience, one must be conscious of all the secondary audiences that exist for one's communication. The primary audience for a company's annual report is shareholders. But two very significant secondary audiences are company workers and the financial community. Most companies are well aware of that fact and tailor their reports accordingly.

This need to anticipate all possible audiences extends into much less obvious situations—writing simple internal memos, for instance. Remember to write them with an eye toward those who will be sent copies as well as to the primary recipient. And also think about who beyond that list might see the memo: the boss's boss? a competitor? government lawyers involved in some sort of routine investigation of the company three years down the road?

The possible existence of many secondary audiences is one reason for being sure to go beyond, "What do I want to say?" Cover, "What should I say?" before issuing any significant communication.

ADOPTING THE APPROPRIATE TONE

An effective manager must adopt the appropriate tone to communicate effectively to different audiences. One must speak to an assembly-line worker in a way that is clear and relevant to that individual. To get across the exact same message to a board of directors will require a dramatically different approach. The words must be right for each audience, and so must the tone, or personality, of the communication.

Advertising experts call this getting the "brand personality" of an advertising campaign right, so that it communicates clearly to its target audience. Heineken ads have an elitist tone that is appropriate for a very expensive, imported beer. Miller Lite ads are humorous and anything but snobbish, befitting a less-expensive brand that is trying to appeal to most American beer drinkers.

The element of tone in the communication between communicator and audience must be examined with regard to the level of expertise each has. The communication may be directed from generalist to generalist, generalist to specialist, specialist to specialist, or from specialist to generalist.

The approach that may be necessary to gain credibility with an audience of generalists may totally ruin credibility with an audience of specialists, and vice versa.

MANAGEMENT COMMUNICATIONS EXERCISES

As mentioned earlier, HBS students don't just talk about how they would attack complex MC problems. Students take their best shot at writing the memo or issuing the report or giving the speech to address the issues raised in the case. As in real life, the amount of time allowed to develop the assigned communication is limited, usually to a few days. Once one's communication is presented, one gets strong feedback on how it could have been improved.

Many different communication exercises are used throughout the course. Students write several memoranda on different topics to different audiences, and a number of longer reports. At least one major group-writing assignment is included each year. Press releases, termination notices, and job-application letters are also required.

HBSers pay particular attention to that last-mentioned exercise. The many first-year students whose written request for an interview is rejected by a prospective consulting firm or investment bank often look again at their covering letters and notice subtle errors in style and/or content that might well have hurt their causes.

Students give at least one major speech during the course and may also participate in numerous in-class speaking exercises.

Translation of theory to action via the exercises, however painful it seems at the time, is an important element in HBS's program to graduate managers that can communicate as well as analyze.

BEYOND THEORY AND EXERCISES

Strong communication takes more than intelligence, analysis, and hard work. A communicator must also strive to offer the audience the following:

- Smart, interesting ideas. It's hard to make an Everest of a communication out of a mole-hillish idea.
- Real conviction behind the communication. It is hard to be brilliant while waffling.
- A relaxed presentation. Knowing the material, having good ideas and a comfortable style all help.
- Honesty in the communication. Frankness is refreshing and infectious, and HBS isn't the only place in the world with too much BS.
- A sensibility to the audience's interests, concerns, likes and fears.
- At least a little humor.

Incisive communication is a major responsibility of management, and can be one of its most powerful tools.

Great communication is an art as well as a science. The MC course at HBS teaches students who care to listen a little bit about both.

MANAGEMENT COMMUNICATIONS CHECKLIST

To quickly assess one's management communication skills as well as those of a company as a whole, consider the following questions:

1. Is effective management communication awarded a high priority?
2. Are all the issues clearly thought through before a given communication is attempted?
3. Are communications clear and concise?
4. Do communications answer all the important questions at hand?
5. Are communications appropriately tailored to address all possible audiences?
6. Does each communication have the proper tone, as well as the correct content?
7. Does the information being communicated have style, substance, conviction, honesty, and humor?

10

BUSINESS, GOVERNMENT, AND THE INTERNATIONAL ECONOMY

In our chapter on Business Policy, we stated that BP is the course in which HBS students look at the big, big picture. If BP looks at the big, big picture, then Business, Government, and the International Economy (Big E) looks at the big, big, *big* picture. Big E looks at the global economy, with emphasis on the analysis of individual countries' economic strategies, and resulting economic performance.

Big E is a course most students find interesting, although some find it frustrating. In addition to cases that include voluminous amounts of numbers (usually historical economic data) to be analyzed, the study of entire nations' economic and political situations seems to many students beyond the scope of the typical general manager's responsibility.

HBS students are aware, however, that management must study and respond to the business environment, current and future, in order to successfully design the corporate ship and guide it safely toward its desired destination. Big E teaches HBS students about the national and international economies in which corporations exist and operate. It teaches future managers to be aware of the ever-changing political, economic, social, and cultural surroundings they operate in; and of the people, institutions, and policies that will shape and reshape those surroundings. One needs only to consider the importance of such issues as what the rate of inflation is likely to be in the future; how fast the U.S. and world economies are likely to grow; what new taxes are likely; what actions from Japan, Korea, or European competitors need to be anticipated; or what form of government trade restrictions are likely, to see the importance of Big E issues in managers' planning and policy making.

The first half of Big E focuses on comparative analysis of the national strategies and performance of Canada, Japan, the United States, Germany, France, and the United Kingdom.

Several historical periods are examined for each, with the greatest attention focused on the United States and its greatest challenger for world economic leadership, Japan. All cases in this first segment are pre-1971. They examine individual economies and also give HBS students a coherent picture of the economy of the industrialized world and its basic trade and monetary systems before 1971.

The students are then made aware of the many changes that came about in the early 1970s that shook the foundations of the international economy and began setting the stage for a dramatically different economic environment in which companies would be forced to compete in the 1970s and beyond. Those changes included:

- The abrogation of the Bretton Woods agreement and fixed rates of exchange for national currencies
- The end of the post-World War II era when growth and resources in the industrial world seemed almost unlimited and growth per se was regarded as good

- The beginning of a period of rising energy prices and worldwide dependence on hitherto powerless oil-producing countries
- The end of an international political and economic system in which U.S. leadership was widely recognized and, often, taken for granted
- The emergence of Japan as a second major contender for the throne of world economic leadership; the rise of the Common Market; the emergence of the economies of many developing countries
- The increasing globalization of the political-economic environment, brought about by improvements in communication and transportation, and accelerated by the global economic strategies adopted by certain nations and corporations

Managers of the 1980s and beyond, regardless of the nation they call home or business they are in, must recognize these changes, and must plan for and capitalize on them if their companies are to succeed.

The second half of the Big E course focuses on the causes of those changes, among others, their impact on business, and certain nations' responses to them. Besides undertaking current-history analyses by country, cases focus on the world-energy supply system, the world trade situation, and the international banking system. The special troubles faced by debt-burdened developing nations are also examined in Big E.

The course ends with a look at the current economic environment and national policies of Japan and the United States, and a discussion of the issues and opportunities each faces in the decade to come. Case studies on developing economies, such as Mexico, South Korea, and Brazil, are also examined.

To learn the lessons of Big E, HBSers attack cases and instructional notes that are among HBS's longest and most number laden. If called on to open a Big E case about the rebirth of the Japanese economy after World War II, a case that included forty pages of text and twenty pages of numerical exhibits, even Quantitative Analysis Jocks who cruised through Finance and Marketing were known to consider resorting to the famous "Beam me up, Scotty" ploy.

Being an obsessive number cruncher may actually be a considerable detriment to doing well on the Big E exams or in class discussions. Big E cases are like many real-world management situations in which there are too many different numbers to analyze them all in any reasonable period of time, and most such analysis would be worthless anyway. The student who can quickly eyeball the overall picture, key in on the important issues, and then crunch only the four or five relevant sets of numbers needed to answer the most immediate questions is the one who excels in Big E. Synthesizers and Political Animals seem to do particularly well in the course.

Learning how to eyeball the numbers is an important lesson. Executives who are considered unusually intelligent are often the ones who can walk into a strategy session where thirty charts are up on the wall, or come upon an exhibit containing 500 numbers, and within seconds spot an error or pinpoint a critical issue revealed in the data. HBS students have to learn to eyeball the numbers on Big E exhibits to spot trends and illustrate key issues—or risk being hopelessly lost in the numbers throughout the course.

They are left with a clear sense that managers in American corporations and those abroad must learn at least to eyeball the political and economic environment of their nation and the world. Only the largest companies will have specialists to do this, but it is an element of looking to the future and setting effective corporate strategies that every business should undertake.

THE BIG E DECISION-MAKER

In Big E cases the decision-making roles HBS students take on are somewhat different than the positions taken in the case studies used in other first-year courses.

In most Big E cases, students are not asked to consider the

situation of a particular business manager. Instead, they evaluate the performance and policies of an entire nation, trying to recommend future actions to help that nation achieve its goals. Positions aren't specified in the cases, but the point of view students assume is that of a nation's leader, like Ronald Reagan; a presidential advisor, like David Stockman; and others who affect national policy, such as a congressman, a lobbyist; or a business executive.

What is surprising to many HBS students is that running a country is very much like running a huge business. Successful leaders must undertake constant analysis of situations and review of relevant options. They must set effective and consistent policies; exercise strong management of the government bureaucracy, and maintain constant communication with important constituents in order to build their confidence and enlist their support.

A few Big E cases do put HBSers into the shoes of particular corporations confronted with Big E issues.

Zenith Corporation is one example. Students study Zenith managers' responses when faced with sharply increased imports of Japanese television sets into the United States.

Other interesting roles the Big E cases put HBS students into include the following:

- Leaders of U.S. oil giants managing relationships with Mideast leaders from the 1940s through the early 1970s, leading up to the rise to power of the Organization of Petroleum Exporting Countries (OPEC)
- Representatives of the International Monetary Fund (IMF) considering what economic and political actions to demand from borrowing nations in return for granting low-interest loans
- David Stockman, former Reagan Administration budget director, just before and just after publication of his famous interview in *Atlantic* magazine.

When class discussion of the Stockman article began, the first few speakers echoed the sentiment probably held by most

Americans—that some of the more interesting statements quoted in the article "somehow leaked out" of Stockman, that he was "embarrassed," that Reagan "took him to the woodshed," and that the budget director would move ahead with his work, wounded but still supported by a forgiving President.

By the time class discussion ended, many students had an increased awareness that few things ever "leak" out in Washington; that Stockman probably made a conscious decision, after consultation with a number of associates, to speak with William Greider, the reporter who wrote the article; and that a lot of other players in the budget process, such as congressmen, lobbyists, and military leaders, were left probably more exposed and embarrassed than Stockman. Who knows whether Reagan paddled Stockman out in the woodshed or congratulated him on an Oscar performance playing the heavy for a naive administration.

Whether studying Stockman, Japan, or the IMF, HBS students become aware that managers in every business have a responsibility to analyze the national and international political and economic environment they compete in as they plan their company's future. Educated guesses about future growth, interest rates, competition, and a host of other factors are critical components of any sound strategic plan and need to be made continually.

Students also gain heightened awareness of the need for all citizens to understand how government strategies and policies affect the economy in order to participate fully in the process. Every voter is in effect a Big E decision-maker.

THE IMPORTANCE OF BIG E DECISIONS

HBS students learn just how important those Big E decisions are for each nation's citizens, businesses, and trading partners.

Japan's rise from ruin after World War II to a position of international economic leadership, despite an almost total lack of natural resources, is the most dramatic example of the impact Big E-style decision-makers have on their country's performance. Japanese policies have slowly but surely built an international economic powerhouse with great benefits for almost every Japanese citizen and business. These same policies have resulted in a disastrous competitive disadvantage for many non-Japanese businesses whose managers failed to study the emerging Japanese competition and devise appropriate responses.

Japan's spectacular and unabating economic growth, low unemployment, low interest rates, high savings and investment rates, strong export industry, and constantly increasing productivity are testimony to intelligent management of the Japanese economy. In contrast, U.S. economic performance, though unquestionably strong in many ways over a long period of time, has shown increasing inconsistency since the early 1960s.

Speak with the average U.S. auto worker, steel worker, shipbuilder, or shoe manufacturer and some of the very tangible, painful results of infirm economic management will be made clear. Ask businessmen and consumers who weathered 20 percent interest rates and they will leave little doubt that there is much to be gained by improving the Big E decision-making of government and business in the United States.

BIG E ANALYSIS

HBS stresses that the national and international economic environment must be analyzed systematically to be understood and properly managed.

ANALYTIC PRINCIPLES

Big E analysis rests on several principles as stated in the Big E course outline:

1. The nation state is a useful unit of environmental analysis, and the behavior of one nation can be better understood if it is compared with that of others.

2. Nations have strategies—overall goals, and policies put in place to achieve those goals—that are explicitly or implicitly defined by governments. These strategies can be analyzed historically and used as a way of thinking about the future.

3. The actions of national governments are the most important influence on the business environment. In order to analyze this environment and to understand the pressures and constraints that limit one's actions, it is useful for the student to take the point of view of a top government policy-maker.

4. Transnational systems are also important to an understanding of the business environment. The flow of energy, money, and trade among nations, for example, and the institutions that govern this flow—such as OPEC, international banks, the IMF, and the General Agreement of Tariffs and Trade (GATT)—are critical components of the business environment and must also be analyzed.

COUNTRY ANALYSIS FRAMEWORK

To aid them in accomplishing the objectives of the course, the students are taught a simple but powerful framework for understanding the complicated economic, political, and social data available about any nation. HBS's "country analysis" is not a model or theory of economic performance; it is simply a framework for organizing available information, and for identifying and then analyzing some of the major options confronting any nation's economic policy-makers at any given period in history.

Four sequential steps are taken in doing a thorough country analysis.

Step One
Analyze a country's current economic performance.

Step Two
Identify a country's current strategy—a government's goals and the policies it has in place. HBS students learn to draw relationships between the policies that are being used and the elements of economic performance identified in Step One.

Step Three
Analyze a country's context—the domestic and international constraints and opportunities that influence the making and maintaining of goals and policy decisions. Again, HBS students learn to relate each step to the ones before it.

Step Four
Make recommendations that best take into account the current performance, strategy, and context of the country.

A premium is placed on HBS students' recommendations being realistic, given all of the parties and politics involved in government decision-making. It's easy to sit in Aldrich Hall or Toledo or Dallas and say Ronald Reagan should cut the federal budget deficit. It is another thing entirely to develop workable strategy for accomplishing that.

To see how the students learn to analyze national economic performance, let's use HBS's example of the United States in January 1973. The case outlines in about fifteen pages (not counting exhibits) the message that Richard Nixon delivered to the American people in his 1973 inaugural address—following one of the greatest election landslides in the country's history—to the effect that his tough but sound management of the U.S. economy had licked inflation, restored growth and put the country back on the road to prosperity.

Your goal in doing the country analysis: to examine the available data and decide whether Nixon deserves the credit he claimed; to determine the actions one could likely expect from his administration in his second term, and what economic performance would be likely to follow.

PERFORMANCE ANALYSIS

A typical HBS case presented for analysis may include the following exhibits—data available to any U.S. citizen through various government announcements and reports.

1. gross national product or expenditure in 1958 dollars
   implicit price deflators for gross national product
   changes in consumer price indexes, commodities, and
   services
2. selected unemployment rates
3. industrial production indexes, selected manufacturers
4. manufacturing output, capacity and utilization rate
5. money stock measures
6. bond yields and interest rates
7. federal budget receipts, outlays, financing and debt
8. U.S. balance of payments
9. international economic comparisons:
   economic profile, 1972
   world trade: exports
   world trade: imports
   trends in productivity and wage earnings in manufacturing
   U.S. foreign trade trends:
   agricultural products
   minerals and fuels
   manufactured products
   U.S. trade with:
   Canada
   E.E.C. (European Economic Community)
   Japan
   LDCs (Less developed countries)
10. petroleum statistics:
    share of imports in U.S. domestic petroleum demand
    average annual well-head price of U.S. crude oil
    key foreign oil price postings

Those exhibits might amount to twenty pages of numbers. Obviously, experience and judgment are needed to know where to start and what to analyze. Many HBS students begin their analysis with an examination of trends in the various components of the nation's gross national product—a figure compiled by the U.S. Commerce Department and designed to summarize the total economic activity of the country on a quarterly and annual basis.

Figure 10–1 is an example of a GNP exhibit for the period 1960–1972. Annual numbers are included for each year. Seasonally adjusted annual rates by quarter are included for only the most recent years to enable closer analysis of activity during the final three full years of the Nixon administration.

From analysis of the total GNP trend, note that total GNP did indeed grow at 6.5 percent in 1972 but that GNP growth in the 1969–1971 period was very low; in fact, the average growth in that period was the lowest in any three-year period since the Depression. The U.S. GNP actually declined in 1970, the first year that Nixon's economic policies took full effect. Yes, the economy was on an upswing in 1972—a reelection year—but life was none too good under Nixon for the first three years.

From analysis of the internal GNP components, students would notice that the Nixon administration had dramatically reduced total government spending in the economy in 1969, 1970, and 1971, which seemed to have significantly slowed and depressed economic growth during the 1969–71 period. Nixon had been practicing very restrictive fiscal policy up until election year. In 1972, he boosted government spending.

Analysis of the U.S. money supply data shows that the Federal Reserve had been restricting growth in the nation's money supply at the same time. That monetary policy, which was encouraged by the Nixon administration, combined with restraining fiscal policies, threw the brakes on the U.S. economy in the 1969–71 period.

In addition, the Nixon administration was experimenting with price controls and import restrictions. Yet, analysis of the GNP reveals that inflation was at about the same level in 1972 as it had been in the year before Nixon's election, and import growth was again far exceeding the growth in U.S. exports in 1972.

This analysis raises some serious questions about the credit Nixon was claiming in his 1972 speech. Yes, some signals on the economic front were looking positive in 1972–73, but they were positive only in relation to the depressed years Nixon's administration engineered via restraining fiscal and monetary policy in 1969–71. Were the moves Nixon made to stimulate the economy in 1972 only effective election-year politicking, or had his tight economic policies helped cure some of the nation's economic ills during the three years of tough times?

In pondering the lessons of the case, HBS students would be mindful of the nature of Japan's economy, and the results of its policies. Japanese economic policy is directed consistently (and successfully) toward moving Japan ahead economically, and is not manipulated to win elections.

Analysis of figure 10–2 would lead to observations that unemployment was on a slow downward trend in 1972, but that far more Americans were unemployed in 1972 than when Nixon took office in 1968.

Analysis of other exhibits (not supplied here) would reveal to students that—

1. The Federal budget deficit was growing rapidly again in 1972 and 1973.
2. American factories' utilization rate was down to 77.6 percent in 1972, as against 87.9 percent in 1967.
3. The U.S. trade deficit was accelerating.
4. The growth in productivity of the average U.S. worker was only about one-third that of the Japanese worker counterpart, just as it had been when Nixon took office.

In sum, many HBS students would conclude that the economic gains Nixon was claiming as the election neared in 1972 were impressive only compared to the depressed years

FIGURE 10–1.
BGIE CASE EXHIBIT

—Gross national product or expenditure in 1958 dollars

Year or quarter	Total gross national product	Personal consumption expenditures					Gross private domestic investment					
		Total	Durable goods	Non-durable goods	Services	Total	Fixed Investment					Change in business inventories
							Total	Nonresidential			Residential structures	
								Total	Structures	Producers' durable equipment		
Billions of 1958 dollars												
1960	487.7	316.1	44.9	149.6	121.6	72.4	68.9	47.1	17.4	29.6	21.9	3.5
1961	497.2	322.5	43.9	153.0	125.6	69.0	67.0	45.5	17.4	28.1	21.6	2.0
1962	529.8	338.4	49.2	158.2	131.1	79.4	73.4	49.7	17.9	31.7	23.8	6.0
1963	551.0	353.3	53.7	162.2	137.4	82.5	76.7	51.9	17.9	34.0	24.8	5.8
1964	581.1	373.7	59.0	170.3	144.4	87.8	81.9	57.8	19.1	38.7	24.2	5.8
1965	617.8	397.7	66.6	178.6	152.5	99.2	90.1	66.3	22.3	44.0	23.8	9.0
1966	658.1	418.1	71.7	187.0	159.4	109.3	95.4	74.1	24.0	50.1	21.3	13.9
1967	675.2	430.1	72.9	190.2	167.0	101.2	93.5	73.2	22.6	50.6	20.4	7.7
1968	706.6	452.7	81.3	197.1	174.4	105.2	98.8	75.6	23.4	52.2	23.2	6.4
1969	725.6	469.1	85.6	201.3	182.2	110.5	103.8	80.1	24.3	55.8	23.7	6.7
1970	722.1	477.0	83.1	207.0	186.8	104.0	99.9	77.6	23.6	54.0	22.3	4.1
1971	741.7	495.4	92.1	211.1	192.2	108.6	105.9	76.8	22.8	54.0	29.1	2.6
1972	789.7	524.8	103.1	220.5	201.2	123.8	119.3	84.3	22.9	61.3	35.0	4.5
Seasonally adjusted annual rates												
1970: I ...	720.4	474.1	83.8	204.4	185.9	102.0	101.0	78.8	24.0	54.8	22.2	0.9
II..	723.2	476.9	84.7	206.0	186.2	105.6	100.0	78.9	23.9	55.0	21.1	5.6
III..	726.8	480.2	84.9	207.7	187.6	106.2	101.3	79.3	23.5	55.7	22.0	4.9
IV..	718.0	476.5	78.9	209.9	187.8	102.2	97.4	73.6	22.9	50.7	23.9	4.8
1971: I ...	731.9	488.2	88.8	210.0	189.3	105.0	101.2	75.3	23.4	51.9	25.9	3.8
II...	737.9	493.0	90.0	211.2	191.8	110.0	104.7	76.4	23.0	53.3	28.3	5.3
III..	742.5	497.4	94.2	210.5	192.8	107.3	106.6	76.4	22.5	53.9	30.1	.7
IV..	754.5	503.2	95.4	212.8	195.0	112.0	111.3	79.2	22.2	57.0	32.1	.7
1972: I ...	766.5	511.0	98.6	214.7	197.7	116.6	116.3	82.2	23.0	59.2	34.2	.3
II...	783.9	520.9	100.7	220.1	200.0	122.0	118.0	83.6	23.0	60.6	34.4	3.9
III..	796.1	528.7	104.5	221.9	202.3	125.5	119.3	84.2	22.6	61.6	35.1	6.2
IV..	812.4	538.6	108.4	225.3	204.9	131.1	123.4	87.2	23.1	64.0	36.3	7.7

his policies brought on through the first three years of his administration, and that the gains hid many severe underlying weaknesses that were developing in the U.S. economy.

The underlying health of the U.S. manufacturing industry had not improved over the first four years of the Nixon administration, and great vulnerabilities to foreign competition,

—Gross national product or expenditure in 1958 dollars (continued)

Year or quarter	Net exports of goods and services			Government purchases of goods and services[1]			Addendum: Gross private product	Percent change from preceding period[2]	
	Net exports	Exports	Imports	Total	Federal	State and local		Total gross national product	Gross private product
Billions of 1958 dollars									
1960........	4.3	27.3	23.0	94.9	51.4	43.5	444.0	2.5	2.4
1961........	5.1	28.0	22.9	100.5	54.6	45.9	452.3	1.9	1.9
1962........	4.5	30.0	25.5	107.5	60.0	47.5	482.9	6.6	6.7
1963........	5.6	32.1	26.6	109.6	59.5	50.1	503.2	4.0	4.2
1964........	8.3	36.5	28.2	111.2	58.1	53.2	532.0	5.4	5.7
1965........	6.2	37.4	31.2	114.7	57.9	56.8	567.0	6.3	6.6
1966........	4.2	40.2	36.1	126.5	65.4	61.1	603.5	6.5	6.4
1967........	3.6	42.1	38.5	140.2	74.7	65.5	617.5	2.6	2.3
1968........	1.0	45.7	44.7	147.7	78.1	69.6	647.0	4.7	4.8
1969........	.2	48.4	48.3	145.9	73.5	72.4	664.9	2.7	2.8
1970........	2.2	52.2	50.0	139.0	64.7	74.3	661.3	−.5	−.5
1971........	.1	52.6	52.5	137.6	60.8	76.8	681.0	2.7	3.0
1972........	−1.8	56.9	58.7	142.9	61.6	81.3	728.4	6.5	6.9
Seasonally adjusted annual rates									
1970: I	1.9	51.9	50.0	142.4	69.0	73.5	659.5	−2.5	−2.6
II	2.0	52.3	50.4	138.6	64.8	73.8	662.3	1.5	1.7
III	2.9	52.4	49.5	137.5	62.9	74.6	666.1	2.0	2.3
IV	1.9	52.1	50.1	137.3	62.1	75.1	657.4	−4.8	−5.1
1971: I	2.7	53.0	50.3	136.1	60.2	75.9	671.3	8.0	8.7
II	−.7	53.0	53.8	135.7	59.7	76.0	677.5	3.4	3.7
III	.1	54.4	54.3	137.6	61.0	76.7	681.7	2.5	2.5
IV	−1.8	49.9	51.7	141.1	62.3	78.8	693.7	6.7	7.2
1972: I	−3.3	55.5	58.9	142.2	62.8	79.4	705.6	6.5	7.1
II	−2.8	54.2	57.0	143.9	63.7	80.3	723.0	9.4	10.2
III	−.7	57.2	57.9	142.6	60.8	81.8	734.5	6.3	6.5
IV	−.3	60.5	60.8	143.0	59.2	83.8	750.3	8.5	8.9

[1] Net of Government sales.
[2] Changes are based on unrounded data and therefore may differ slightly from those obtained from published data.

Source: Department of Commerce, Bureau of Economic Analysis.

inflation, and increased interest rates existed. Clearly evident were the underlying problems of outdated plants and equipment, reduced productivity gains, low rates of investment, and high costs that limited export opportunities.

These signs of weakness were visible to careful government and business observers long before the OPEC oil crisis and the intensifying Japanese manufacturing challenge exposed them to the American public and the rest of the world. The

FIGURE 10-2
BGIE CASE EXHIBIT

—Selected unemployment rates

(Percent)

Year or month	All workers	By sex and age			By color		By selected groups					Labor force time lost[4]
		Both sexes 16–29 years	Men 20 years and over	Women 20 years and over	White	Negro and other races	Experienced wage and salary workers	Household heads	Married men[1]	Full-time workers[3]	Blue-collar workers[2]	
1960	5.5	14.7	4.7	5.1	4.9	10.2	5.7	. . . .	3.7	. . . .	7.8	6.7
1961	6.7	16.8	5.7	6.3	6.0	12.4	6.8	. . . .	4.6	6.7	9.2	8.0
1962	5.5	14.7	4.6	5.4	4.9	10.9	5.6	. . . .	3.6	. . . .	7.4	6.7
1963	5.7	17.2	4.5	5.4	5.0	10.8	5.5	3.7	3.4	5.5	7.3	6.4
1964	5.2	16.2	3.9	5.2	4.6	9.6	5.0	3.2	2.8	4.9	6.3	5.8
1965	4.5	14.8	3.2	4.5	4.1	8.1	4.3	2.7	2.4	4.2	5.3	5.0
1966	3.8	12.8	2.5	3.8	3.4	7.3	3.5	2.2	1.9	3.5	4.2	4.2
1967	3.8	12.8	2.3	4.2	3.4	7.4	3.6	2.1	1.8	3.4	4.4	4.2
1968	3.6	12.7	2.2	3.8	3.2	6.7	3.4	1.9	1.6	3.1	4.1	4.0
1969	3.5	12.2	2.1	3.7	3.1	6.4	3.3	1.8	1.5	3.1	3.9	3.9
1970	4.9	15.2	3.5	4.8	4.5	8.2	4.8	2.9	2.6	4.5	6.2	5.3
1971	5.9	16.9	4.4	5.7	5.4	9.9	5.7	3.6	3.2	5.5	7.4	6.4
1972	5.6	16.2	4.0	5.4	5.0	10.0	5.3	3.3	2.8	5.1	6.5	6.0
Seasonally adjusted												
1972: Jan . .	5.9	17.5	4.2	5.6	5.3	10.6	5.6	3.5	3.0	5.4	7.1	6.4
Feb . .	5.8	18.5	4.1	5.1	5.1	10.5	5.4	3.3	2.8	5.3	7.0	6.1
Mar . .	5.9	17.4	4.2	5.5	5.3	10.5	5.5	3.4	2.8	5.4	6.9	6.3
Apr . .	5.8	16.7	4.2	5.4	5.4	9.6	5.3	3.4	2.9	5.4	6.8	6.3
May . .	5.8	15.7	4.1	5.7	5.3	10.7	5.5	3.6	2.9	5.6	6.8	6.3
June .	5.5	14.9	4.0	5.6	5.0	9.4	5.0	3.6	2.9	5.0	6.4	5.5
July . .	5.6	15.5	3.9	5.7	5.0	9.9	5.3	3.3	2.7	5.1	6.4	6.0
Aug . .	5.6	16.7	3.9	5.5	5.1	9.7	5.3	3.3	2.6	5.1	6.5	6.2
Sept . .	5.5	16.2	3.8	5.4	5.0	10.2	5.2	3.3	2.8	5.0	6.1	5.9
Oct . .	5.5	15.4	3.9	5.5	5.0	10.1	5.2	3.4	2.8	5.0	5.9	6.0
Nov . .	5.2	15.6	3.5	5.0	4.6	9.8	4.9	2.9	2.4	4.6	5.8	5.4
Dec . .	5.1	15.7	3.4	5.1	4.6	9.6	4.9	2.9	2.4	4.7	5.7	5.4

[1]Married men living with their wives. Data for 1949 and 1951–54 are for April; 1950, for March.

[2]Data for 1949–61 are for May.

[3]Includes craftsmen, operatives, and nonfarm laborers. Data for 1948–57 are based on data for January, April, July, and October.

[4]Man-hours lost by the unemployed and persons on part-time for economic reasons as a percent of potentially available labor force man-hours.

Seasonally adjusted data in the first four columns of this table have been revised and do not agree with those published beginning February 1972. They are subject to correction when the annual official revision of the series is published.

Source: Department of Labor, Bureau of Labor Statistics.

lack of concerted action had a great cost for the U.S. consumer and for many U.S. manufacturing workers.

STRATEGY ANALYSIS

After learning how a country's economy is performing, HBS students then try to understand the nature of the government's strategy for running the nation's economy. Careful analysis and plenty of judgment combine to reveal that every nation has a strategy for success that includes goals and policies designed to try to obtain those goals.

In the Nixon case, his administration seemed to have many very popular long-term goals, including lower inflation, increased U.S. productivity, and improved balance of trade. The administration also had one short-term goal of absolute top priority—getting reelected. That included making sure that the press and the electorate saw the country's economic performance in 1972 as favorable.

Did Nixon's short-term goal to get reelected take precedence, and negatively affect his efforts to achieve his long-term goals? HBSers could debate this question forever.

CONTEXT ANALYSIS

As well as gaining an understanding of a country's performance and the strategy that drives it, HBS students learn to consider carefully the context in which decisions are being made. Such thinking often yields clues about which future actions seem likely and which are highly unlikely given the politics, the timing, and the personalities involved in any situation.

In Nixon's case, his 1969–71 actions were understandable given his conservative, Republican background, his campaign promises, and the nation's paranoia about inflation. In context, his 1972 actions probably came as no surprise to careful observers, as they watched Nixon and other Republicans battle to win reelection in a nation that had not reelected a GOP president in sixteen years.

RECOMMENDATIONS FOR THE FUTURE

Looking at the past seems easy. Looking into the future seems, and is, difficult. Looking into the economic future of any nation, especially one driven by political elections every two years, is nearly impossible. Many of the brightest, most highly paid people on earth sit on Wall Street all their lives and fail miserably at predicting the American economy.

HBS doesn't pretend to teach students how to predict the future. The school does teach them—through case analysis, class discussion, and exams—to put together performance, strategy, and context analysis in order to identify the trends, the problems, and the politics of any economic situation. All that enables the students to at least consider what some of the major decision options are, and what an educated guess may indicate about government actions.

Students also get a sense, from studying many different countries, of why policies must fit together to be effective, and of how they can be managed with an eye toward the long term in order to realize maximum success.

HBS students are encouraged to look into many areas when examining the context in which decisions must be made. The cycle of elections and party politics is only one important area to explore.

The location of a nation, its size, population density, and access to raw materials are other important areas. Japan's economic strategy has clearly been dictated by a need to import raw materials and export finished goods in large quantities so it can feed its people and keep its balance of payments manageable.

A nation's social and ideological norms are also critical. Japan's work ethic has played a key role in its strategy. Americans' spirit of independence and innovation has a lot to do with the country's free market and low government involvement in the economy.

The structures and institutions existing within a nation are also important components to be examined. The government, banking system, agricultural system, educational system, labor unions, and major religious groups all influence who will make decisions, what their goals will be, what policies will be put in place, and what kind of economic performance can be expected.

A company's international relationships also will dramatically affect its economic strategy and performance. The day the United States cut off trade with Japan would be a massively disruptive one for Japan, America, and the world. The day Cuba and the United States restored economic trading would be a day of enormous new opportunities and strategic options for Cuba.

BIG E 365 DAYS A YEAR

As we mentioned at the beginning of this chapter, Big E involves looking at the big, big, big picture to better understand the national and international economic environment. Business benefits from Big E analysis in countless ways—by having an informal forecast of future national economic growth and inflation levels, pending legislation, and world trade and interest rate trends. The list of benefits a company receives from improved understanding of the macroeconomic environment is almost endless.

Because we read about or come face-to-face with Japanese imports almost daily, we need to understand what Japan's national economic strategy is; and how its government, banks, corporations, international trade organizations, and workers cooperate to achieve steady economic growth through exports in key industries. In many ways, it is scary how few Americans understand how Japan operates and what to expect from it in the future. The Japanese, on the other hand, are committed to understanding in great detail how American industry and the American government work so that they can continue to sell their goods here in ever increasing quantities.

Closer to home, we read about and come face-to-face with decisions being made in Washington and state capitals each day that affect our economic future.

How likely is it that the second-term Reagan administration can really succeed in cutting the budget deficit? What is the probability of reinstating in 1986 or beyond legislation that restricts Japanese auto imports? What would the odds have been if the U.S. auto manufacturers had put more dollars into plant modernization and less into profits and bonuses in 1983 and 1984? Are the probabilities of import quotas in the steel industry different than in the shoe industry?

The newspapers were awash with articles about how Paul Volcker began to ease the reins on the money supply in the second and third quarters of 1985. What are the implications of this for mortgage interest rates?

Big E issues surround us every day. HBS teaches students to be aware of their existence, and provides a framework for systematically analyzing them. The country analysis framework, combined with an understanding of the comparative economic structure and performance of many nations around the world during different periods in history, gives HBS students a valuable set of tools for understanding the environment in which they are doing business and the options they must be prepared for in the future.

BIG E CHECKLIST

When one considers whether a company is aware of and competently dealing with BGIE issues, the following brief checklist of questions is helpful:

1. Is anyone from the company responsible for analyzing the national and international economic environment in order to—
   Inform management of trends it should be aware of in formulating plans
   Identify any opportunities arising from likely local, state, or federal legislation.
2. Does company planning seem to be taking advantage of national and international economic and political trends, or does it seem to be fighting those trends?

AFTERWORD

INTERVIEWING: AND WHY DO YOU WANT TO WORK FOR US?

After two years of sleepless nights and chronic eye fatigue; of class sessions in which eighty-four so-called classmates re-create the dynamics of a lynch mob; after two years of these and other sundry HBS ordeals, there isn't much that will faze a graduate from the country's most prestigious business school. Not overbearing bosses, contentiously competitive colleagues, potholes, or long commuter-train rides. Not hurried-hamburger lunches, or five-course dinners, turbulent plane flights or crazy cabdrivers.

Although the HBS graduate generally can't look forward to offbeat or colorfully low-key business situations, he or she does have wonderful and numerous career options available.

The number of doors open to HBS graduates is astounding.

Imagine being twenty-six or twenty-eight years old and having several hundred of the world's finest firms beating a path to one's door, encouraging a job interview, wanting to pay $40,000 or more to start, not including generous moving allowances, exploding bonuses, and all the other perquisites that one thought only professional athletes got.

Name the poison. Marketing? Advertising? Banking? Investment Banking? Consulting? Portfolio Management? Real Estate? Collectibles? Chemicals? Publishing? Small Business? Entrepreneurship? It's all there for the picking.

Name the location. Boston? New England? New York? Texas? Chicago? California? The world?

The options are almost overwhelming.

THE INTERVIEWING GAME

Even in this candy store, many HBS students remain caught up in some of the slightly crazy behavior patterns fostered by two years of HBS courses. It's tempting to explore every option. It's hard to turn down any invitation to dinner at Maison Robert, Grill 23, or Seasons even if one isn't interested in the company picking up the check. Why not pamper the ego by actively collecting offers from every company crazy enough to offer starting salaries of $50,000? Why not try to get at least one offer that includes an exploding bonus, if only to find out what an exploding bonus really is?

There is so much pressure (most of it self-imposed) to use an HBS degree as a ticket to a high-paying, high-prestige, and often high-anxiety position that many HBSers wind up stumbling over themselves and nearly self-destructing during the job interview process.

The greatest pressure at HBS is to get at least one job offer from a major management consulting firm and/or one of the major investment banks—whether its really wanted or not. Watching Bain and McKinsey battle for the rights to one's body is the ultimate HBS ego trip.

HBSers are treated to huge, fancy dinners and nonstop talk of bonuses paid on signing, intellectual challenge, and world travel. Not to mention the salary offers many companies come up with ($50,000–$70,000 to start and promises of $100,000–

$200,000 within three to five years). Is it any wonder that red-blooded capitalist HBSers have a hard time not at least exploring these lucrative opportunities? Such companies are extremely selective about who they hire, further fueling the average HBSer's desire to be selected for one of their offers.

By January of the first year, almost two-thirds of our classmates had thought it over carefully, considered all the options regardless of the money, and had concluded that consulting and/or investment banking were the perfect career choices for them. Life is funny that way.

Whether an accountant, a banker, or a ballplayer before HBS, consulting and investment banking were the logical next career stops. Whether a shoe-in Baker Scholar or a screen survivor, consulting and investment banking were the perfect intellectual environments. Whether a Quantitative Analysis Jock, Synthesizer, Humanist, Political Animal, Skydecker or just a plain Eccentric, consulting firms and investment banks offered the perfect working environment.

HBS students' almost fanatical interest in these fields should not be seen as overt denigration of jobs in other areas, such as manufacturing, insurance, banking, marketing, real estate or small business. It became clear that if Mayor Koch came to HBS to offer students starting salaries of $50,000 to ride the two-man sanitation trucks in New York City and if he managed to make the job sound prestigious, two-thirds of the HBS graduates would quickly put together a pitch explaining why the position of sanitation collector was ideally suited to their background, HBS training, and career goals.

We can hear the interview dialogue now.

"Well, sir, I never seriously considered garbage collection before accccepting my pre-HBS position with The First National Bank of Toledo. But thanks to the tons of knowledge now at my disposal, I realize that the future is in refuse...."

With all of the pressure and all of the running around, second-year HBSers playing the interview game have an uncanny knack for developing foot-in-mouth disease.

THE CONSULTANT

In the 1983 class, one preppy, good-looking male who was much sought after by all the consulting firms developed an especially acute case. Many consulting firms rush to do all of their interviews within the first three or four days of the interviewing season in order to make offers to the best students before someone else snaps them up. As a result, this student, like many others, wound up with several straight days of almost continuous interviews with all the big names in consulting: Bain, McKinsey, Booz Allen, MAC, TBS, and a number of others.

On the third day, all of the firms were conducting their recall rounds of interviews at the Cambridge Hyatt hotel. Our friend spent the day going from one company's suite to another conducting hour-long second and third interviews, with only brief dashes to the lobby in between sessions to check over his notes, get all the names straight and prepare for the next interview.

The scene resembled an upscale Marx Brothers movie, with one wing-tipped, navy-pinstripe-suited candidate leaving each suite by one door while another, almost identically attired candidate came in through another door. Candidates riding up and down in the Hyatt's glass-walled elevators took to turning up trench coat collars and hiding behind briefcases as they zoomed past one company's interview room on the way to another's.

By midafternoon, the interviews were starting to blend together. Every interviewer looked the same: attractive, polished, intelligent, very put together, very cheerful—loved consulting, never worked weekends. All the questions started to sound alike: Why consulting? Why the XYZ company? How does your previous experience with ABC prepare you for consulting? What would you do in such-and-such a situation to prove you are brilliant and worth your $1,000-per-hour billing rate?

Then the inevitable happened. The suite he occupied was

Bain and Company's. The interviewers were "Bainey's." Our friend's objective was to get an offer here.

The question was simple, "Why after HBS do you want to work for *us* instead of any other consulting firm?"

Our friend looked 'em straight in the eye, flashed a warm, natural grin and let rip with his best, "Why I've always wanted to work for McKinsey and Company since I was six" spiel. He began with McKinsey's reputation, moved on to McKinsey's philosophy of doing business, and finished by raving about the great McKinsey people he had met in the interviews he had been to before. The interviewer let the rope reel out, then calmly informed our friend that he was interviewing with Bain and Company. The Bain and Company that everyone else wanted a job with. Next please!

The early exit gave our poor friend a few extra minutes in the lobby to compose himself. Luckily for him, he interviewed next with McKinsey and Company. Since he had just dress-rehearsed his McKinsey routine, that interview went exceptionally well. To this day he is happily employed making megabucks at McKinsey and Company.

THE INVESTMENT BANKER

An exceptionally bright friend of ours made the HBS interviewing hall of fame in the process of landing an investment banking job. He had an A+ undergraduate grade-point average and had received all E's in his hardball money courses at HBS—Finance, Accounting, Capital Markets, and others. He was sure the investment banks would be fighting over his services. He signed himself up to talk with every firm that even sounded like an investment bank and hit the interviewing trail.

Unfortunately, for one reason or another, he struck out— first with the major New York investment banks, then with the Chicago and West Coast companies, and finally with the major regionals. Though undoubtedly one of the very best candidates in the class, he was just a terrible interviewer. He watched in horror as Political Animals, Eccentrics, and even

Humanists who couldn't calculate their way through the pub breakfast line landed $50,000 starting salaries with First Boston, Goldman Sachs, et al., while he worked his way down the list to investment banks no one had ever heard of before.

Finally, there was only one company left, a Baltimore company.

Our friend was so busy getting turned down (one day he actually received four rejection letters and one rejection phone call) that he didn't have time to research his last interview before going in. Though shell-shocked, he went into the interview with high hopes and expectations, because he had gone to college near Baltimore and looked forward to moving back to the area.

As our friend tells it, the first twenty minutes of the interview could not have gone better. The interviewer was young and looked a little like our friend. He was a graduate of a college whose basketball team was a major rival of our friend's alma mater. They had visited each other's fraternities over the years. They both wore tassel loafers and skinny ties, both had entered HBS at age twenty-four and both had easily got E's in HBS Finance. Our friend says he was already beginning to think about asking for a signing bonus—things were going that smoothly.

Then it happened. Our friend and the interviewer got down to business.

"Tell me," the interviewer said, "why T. Rowe Price?"

Knowing there were only a few more minutes to the interview and that he could bullshit about investment banking for hours—and that he didn't know a hoot about T. Rowe Price— our friend quickly outlined a six-to-eight-minute investment banking pitch in his head and took off.

"Before talking specifically about T. Rowe Price, I think it's important for me first to give you an idea why I'm committed to going to work in the investment banking field." Our friend noticed the interviewer's smile fade slightly, but he calmly swept ahead on the wave of his investment banking speech—

why he always wanted to be an investment banker, what he had done at HBS to prove his investment banking skills, and how the other investment banks he was expecting offers from had confirmed his interest in the challenging and exciting field of investment banking. He figured that if he said investment banking one more time, he'd probably have to register with the SEC.

Just as he was about to segue into, "You're probably wondering why a well-known smaller investment bank like T. Rowe Price interests me," the interviewer stood up, slid open the alcove interviewing room door and gestured for him to leave.

"Son," he said, "I'll have you know that T. Rowe Price is not an investment bank, never was an investment bank and doesn't ever want to be an investment bank. In fact, you may be the only person in the world who thinks T. Rowe Price is an investment bank. T. Rowe Price is one of the best known and largest investment-management companies in the country, and if you don't know the difference how the hell did you get into Harvard Business School in the first place?"

The interviewer's screams of "HBS asshole" were still ringing in our friend's ears long after he had left the building and walked across Baker Beach and parked himself in the pub for a couple of cold ones.

Fortunately, our friend overcame his interviewing problems before it was altogether too late and landed an excellent job in the mergers and acquisitions area of an aggressive mid-western company with deep pockets. Since graduation, he has been involved in numerous deals and seems well on his way to a very successful and lucrative career.

THE TOUGH COMPETITION AT STANFORD

Not all of the interviewing horror stories at HBS were authored by HBSers. Many of the companies interviewing at HBS contribute to the zaniness.

One very well-known New York consulting firm secured its

own place in the HBS interviewing hall of fame by devising what affectionately came to be known as the "early warning double ding."

Renowned even before the advent of double-D day for its foresight and efficiency, this company thought ahead and had rejection letters produced by word processor for everyone the company was interviewing at Harvard the week before the interviews were to take place. This seemed to make sense since all those doing the interviews would be holed up in the Cambridge Hyatt for four days with no one to type. The only problem was, no one remembered to tell the secretarial staff to hold the letters for a week before even thinking of mailing any of them. The letters went out and the company rejected everyone from HBS before they were even interviewed. Baker Scholars, candidates the company definitely wanted to hire. Everyone. Rejected.

Adding insult to injury, the word processor had inserted Stanford instead of Harvard in all the appropriate places. They had all enjoyed visiting Stanford and were sorry to say they had to reject us (before interviewing us) because all of our Stanford classmates were so impressive.

THIS OFFER EXPLODES BY BREAKFAST

Is it any wonder that HBS students become interview-crazed when companies recruit the way this one does?

The very first company that came to HBS, in January, 1982, to interview the class of '83 for '82 summer jobs was a very well-known, aggressive New York–based investment bank. It had been pre-recruiting since October by taking hand-picked groups of five or six students out to Boston's fanciest restaurants. The company had made it clear—it was out to get the best.

It was well-known that this company would select only two or three HBSers to receive summer offers. One thousand dollars a week plus summer moving expenses was the rumored salary. Over 200 students sought interviews. Invitations to interview were extended to about 100 HBSers.

The interviews began at 9:00 a.m. in a downtown Boston hotel, even though HBS policy is for companies to interview on campus beginning no earlier than 3:00 p.m., in order to minimize disruption of classes. By 4:00 p.m. the investment bank recruiters had completed the first round of interviews and had contacted a group of about fifteen HBSers and asked— make that *ordered*—them back to downtown Boston for second interviews at 5:00 p.m. A cocktail reception for the fifteen finalists and all of the recruiters followed from about 6:00 to 8:00 p.m.

At midnight, three phones rang on the HBS campus and three lucky HBSers had the honor of receiving the first summer-job offers granted the class of 1983.

The only hitch was, the offers were only good until 7:00 a.m., when the interviewers were scheduled to check out of their hotel and head back to New York.

So much for our class's first exposure to career development at HBS. Less than eighteen hours had elapsed since the opening gun. Three had offers, invalid after seven hours—and don't sleep on it, lest you oversleep. One hundred and ninety-seven others had tasted rejection.

FOUR STRIKES AND YOU'RE OUT

By the time the end of the second-year recruiting draws near, most HBS students have thought their options through, have received at least one or two offers they are excited about, and have learned to laugh at most of the absurdity. It is a good thing the following event took place late in a friend's second year, not at the beginning of his first.

He had a nice offer in hand, but there was a certain consulting firm in Washington, D.C., that he really hoped to get an offer from.

Not only did that desired offer not come through, the company actually contacted him four times to make sure he knew he was rejected.

The first call came the afternoon of the interview. The HBSer thought the interview had gone well, so he was a bit surprised. The man who had interviewed him was on the phone. He was a little apologetic, and hesitant, but our friend read the message loud and clear.

Later that night the phone rang again. It was the interviewer's boss calling to reject the poor guy again, apparently unaware he had already been called. Our friend's hopes soared briefly: Was this second call to be a reversal of the first one? On realizing the situation, the second rejector got embarrassed and flustered, but again the HBSer got the message.

The next day a letter arrived from Washington, officially confirming the two oral rejections received the previous day. Being a positive sort, our friend noted that the letter had traveled all the way to Boston in one business day.

Finally, later that afternoon, our friend switched on his answering machine only to hear a taped message from the previous day's first caller, who was calling now to apologize for any confusion he might have caused by being hesitant the day before and just to remind him, once again, that the decision was final. He was definitely rejected.

As our friend tells it, it was almost a week before the fear of opening his mail or turning on his answering machine subsided.

HBS GRADS' CAREER CHOICES

Despite all the interviewing horror stories, most HBS students do land the jobs they desire. Many even have the good sense to turn down lucrative offers from the investment banks and consulting firms. The table on page 253 shows the fields entered into by the HBS class graduating in 1984.

Consulting and investment banking positions did account for the career choices of 38.9 percent of the 1984 graduating class. It is not surprising that these industries had the highest reported median starting salaries at $52,300 and $45,000, respectively

FIGURE 11-1. Selected Placement Results—MBA Class of 1984

Industry	(Salaries in thousands)			No.	Pct.
	Minimum	Maximum	Median		
Manufacturing				148	25.4
Aerospace, Automotive & Other Transportation	35.5	45.0	40.0	16	2.7
Chemicals & Pharmaceuticals	33.0	55.0	40.0	10	1.7
High Technology & Electronics	30.0	60.0	38.4	68	11.7
Miscellaneous Consumer Goods	20.0	55.0	36.8	23	3.9
Non-Manufacturing				428	73.4
Commercial Banking	18.0	57.3	36.0	25	4.3
Computer-related Services	28.0	40.8	35.7	10	1.7
Consulting	24.0	65.0	52.3	111	19.0
Investment Banking	18.0	55.0	45.0	110	18.9
Real Estate, Construction	18.0	60.0	35.3	54	9.3
Retail Trade	30.0	45.0	38.2	15	2.6
Other Diversified Financial	28.8	75.0	41.9	40	6.9
Highly Diversified	35.0	58.0	40.0	7	1.2
Industry Totals				583	100.0
Function					
Finance	18.0	75.0	44.9	168	28.8
Marketing, Sales	18.0	60.0	38.0	145	24.8
Planning	30.0	55.0	37.5	27	4.7
Project Management/Consulting	18.0	65.0	50.0	153	26.2
Production, Service Operations	33.0	60.0	38.5	21	3.6
Other	30.0	90.0	40.0	58	10.0
				583	100.0

Above table does not list industries entered by fewer than 10 graduates; however, they are included in subtotals and industry totals.

However, the other 61.1 percent of the 1984 HBS class entered a wide variety of industries.

Venture capital, real estate, and various high-technology companies attracted many entrepreneurial students.

Some students enter HBS with a particular interest in a field, like advertising, sales, or management of a family business. Many return to those areas upon graduation. For a number of these students, the decision is to pass up larger starting salaries in consulting or investment banking for earlier management responsibility in an industry in which they have a particular interest.

Still other graduates strike out to start their own businesses.

Among our '83 classmates at least a dozen have opened new enterprises, ranging from a designer dress company in New York, to a publishing business in Los Angeles, to an electronic-components manufacturing company in Mexico. Interest in entrepreneurship is on the rise at HBS, and many sources of advice and capital are open to HBS graduates inclined toward a start-up venture.

In our eyes, these people are the jewels of the HBS crop. They often buck peer pressure in order to do creative things they have wanted to do for a long time, or that they feel will pay off in the long run, rather than rationalizing a decision to go after the big quick bucks in investment banking and consulting. We often wish the HBS system encouraged more people to pursue individual career and life goals, rather than reinforcing what in the past few years has almost become the traditional HBS career path into investment banking and consulting. In some ways, HBS students are losing out because the school is not encouraging its students to be more creative in formulating their post-graduation aspirations, and we fear that in some ways American business is losing out as well when a high percentage of a generation of business leaders are being tacitly trained to view the world in a consulting or advising role, rather than in the role of doing and making things.

This is not meant to say that consulting and investment banking are not worthy pursuits for many individuals. And it is easy to understand why HBS graduates, most of whom traded fairly high-paying jobs for school loans, are attracted to the highest paying opportunities available to them. However, we do question whether these two industries are really the best alternative for almost 40 percent of the very diverse pool of future business leaders who leave Baker Beach each year. That question is asked by many of our fellow HBS students, past and present. It is one we hope the school administrators will consider in the years to come.

THE SOMETIMES HIDDEN COSTS OF HBS

For all one has learned and all of the options one has open upon completion of two years at HBS, one must be aware that the costs of an HBS degree are great. The results of a cost benefit analysis of pursuing an HBS diploma will vary greatly from one individual to another.

The monetary costs of attending HBS are easy to calculate. In 1985–86, the HBS admissions office estimated the total cost of the program at about $24,000 for a first-year student. Tuition was $10,750. The single-student health fee was $650. Case materials cost $850. A Harvard dorm room cost $2,450 to $3,400. All students are strongly encouraged to buy an IBM- or IBM-compatible computer system and software. Students are also encouraged to eat regularly and seek occasional recreation.

Students generally earn $5,000 to $10,000 during the summer between their first and second years. But some of this is eaten up by the three-month binge of lavish living many of these discretionary income-starved people allow themselves.

The nonmonetary costs of attending HBS are harder to calculate, but equally real. One must give up two years of earnings and two years of on-the-job experience and career advancement.

The intense pressure also takes its toll in many ways. Those who fail—and, tragically, 5 to 8 percent of each class will not graduate—can be deeply scarred. Even some of those who complete the program leave HBS less comfortable than they'd like to be with who they are and about what they ultimately want to do with their lives. HBS has a way of permanently raising one's blood pressure and expectations to unusual heights.

Along the way, HBS does not provide a lot of psychological support, career guidance, or life guidance for its students. It is very much the student's own responsibility to withstand the two years of intense pressure and to put that experience to work in a beneficial manner.

Time gets devoured. Expectations get raised. Egos get continually built up, shattered, and built up again. Not surprisingly, many very strong personal relationships end when one party goes off to HBS. And HBS does not foster the forming of new close relationships—of any kind—to take their place.

IS THE HBS DEGREE WORTH THE COST?

Everyone mulling over this question must answer it anew. The high costs demand thorough and thoughtful analysis.

Of course, one can never really answer the question with certainty. Choose HBS, and how will one ever know what might have transpired if the two years on the Charles were passed up? Would one have been more or less successful?

Conclude that the Harvard MBA is unaffordable, and who'll ever know what was missed? Who will ever know how high he or she could have gone?

Kelly and Kelly happen to believe that our two years at HBS will pay off handsomely for us over the long run. As for doing HBS together, well, let's just say we weathered our share of storms.

We both left good jobs to attend HBS but returned to the real world two years later with salaries and responsibility levels at least equal to and probably significantly greater than would have come with two straight years of work experience. In addition, we returned to our careers with the self-confidence of having survived the HBS program, with greatly enhanced perspective, and with all of the HBS learning added to our arsenals. We feel that countless options are open to us in the future should we need or desire them.

In general we think HBS is right for the person who knows where he or she wants to go and who is confident a Harvard MBA will help get there. Or for someone who feels he or she has strong potential in the arena of business management but who needs the training, insight into career alternatives, and access to the higher-level starting positions that an HBS degree offers.

Who isn't HBS right for? That is difficult for us to say. It certainly isn't right for some, but people must judge for themselves.

ARE HBS GRADUATES WORTH IT?

The enormous starting salaries MBAs receive, and the voracious appetite many companies display for HBS graduates, raise the important question that this book has in part tried to answer: What do they really teach at the Harvard Business School that makes an HBS graduate a special person? Why do many of the world's premier companies compete so hotly and pay so dearly for HBS graduates?

Many interrelated ingredients make up the HBS formula: the intelligent and highly motivated student body, the intense HBS environment, the stimulating case-study method, the HBS curriculum, all contribute.

Do you need a Harvard Business School MBA to become a great general manager, investment banker, advertising executive, manufacturing plant manager, or entrepreneur? Of course not!

Two years at HBS helps people to develop further the drive and natural talent they bring to HBS to begin with, and helps them to open doors in order to capitalize on every chance to develop further.

Those who recruit HBS students often learn this the hard way. That a job candidate made it through two years at HBS doesn't mean he or she is right for the job. Look at the HBS person at an interview as if he or she had just arrived from Podunk University Business School. Would you hire *that person*? Does the person have the drive, interest in your business, personality, and instincts that make you willing to pay him or her your hard-earned money? If so, hire that person.

If the person is right for your business and has a Harvard MBA, all the better. He or she is worth a lot of money, because that person will probably work like crazy and perform exceptionally well.

But if you're only hiring the degree, you are not making a wise investment.

HBS students also need to avoid deluding themselves. If you, an HBS student, were not a naturally methodical analyst, a daring trader, or a hard-nosed real estate negotiator before walking into Aldrich Hall, there is no real reason to think you'll be any of those things when you walk out two years later.

An HBS degree doesn't remove your responsibility to understand yourself—your strengths and weaknesses, likes and dislikes—and to find a way of making a living that fits in with your unique makeup and personality. By refusing to fall sway to the peer pressure to make $100,000 within three years of attaining your MBA, you open the way to letting the HBS experience help you follow, confidently and fruitfully, your own instincts.

THE GIFT OF SELF-CONFIDENCE

Maybe the single most important element one acquires through Harvard Business schooling is a sense of great personal satisfaction and self-confidence. Anyone who has been to HBS knows the feeling. Anyone who hasn't but who has read this book can imagine what it is like. Anyone who has tackled a huge challenge successfully can relate to the HBS graduate.

We personally took from HBS a faith that we can figure out the right answer and get the job done in almost any situation. It is the benefit of HBS that we have both commented on more than any other since graduation. Our working-world observation is that a major problem in American business today is that too few people are really hungry to take responsibility for getting important things done. And many of those who are in positions of responsibility and power often seem more afraid to risk failure than they are hungry to aspire to success.

Think of the people you work with. How often does anyone bowl you over by going the extra mile to get a job done without being asked? How many people working for you can you trust 110 percent to get a job done on time and correctly? Not too many, most readers will answer.

Most HBS graduates, on the other hand, even though they may irritate some people in the process, want the responsibility, believe they can get the job done, and have the base of training to know how to attack the problem. It is a way of thinking and feeling—and acting—that can lead to success in almost any industry, anywhere.

THE BOTTOM LINE

Like everything else in life, to a certain extent you get out of Harvard Business School what you put into it. The school will not make a fool into a genius. But neither will it take a compassionate, humane person, and make him or her into an automaton.

HBS is self-selecting to some extent, and on the surface it may seem that all HBSers are alike. But they are not. They run the spectrum from abrasive to soft-spoken, from right-of-Reagan to, well, not quite left-of-Lenin.

Some lack social skills, to be sure, and HBS will not redress that lack. Many couldn't cut a deal to save their lives. Others can feel out a negotiating adversary before the opening handshake is concluded, but need other people to do the analytical support work that allows them to structure a financially viable deal.

A lot of people have sold a lot of books in the past decade telling readers why they don't need to go to business school, what you can't learn there. But the proof is in the pudding, and the top business schools in the country, with Harvard right up there, still consistently turn out some of the most savvy managers in American business. And American business is still flourishing.

There will be changes made at HBS in the next decade, just as there have been changes made in the past. More people-oriented courses have been added, the atmosphere has made concessions—few and far between to be sure—to a growing population of women, nonwhite American and third-world students who attend. And these people have enhanced the HBS experience, bringing a diversity and realism to the scene on the Charles that American managers must face, and take advantage of.

What do they really teach you at the Harvard Business School? A method. A method of looking at the world, for taking a problem and searching your vast mental file drawer of examples to see which ways this problem is similar to any of them. A method of using examples that are similar, yet by no means the same, to extrapolate what a solution might be to the problem at hand. What they teach you at the Harvard Business School is to deal with that problem today, not tomorrow; to deal with it as best you can and not to dwell on it. Because tomorrow there will be another problem, equally baffling, equally challenging, equally possible to solve.

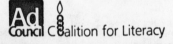